The Welles - Turner Memorial Library
Glastonbury, Connecticut

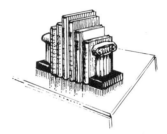

D1636788

SILAS DEANE—

Patriot or Traitor?

S. Deane.

Drawn from the life by Du. Simitier in Philadelphia.   Engraved by B. L. Prevost at Paris.

SILAS DEANE–

Patriot or Traitor?

COY HILTON JAMES

MICHIGAN STATE UNIVERSITY PRESS

1975

Copyright © 1975
MICHIGAN STATE UNIVERSITY PRESS
Library of Congress Card Catalog Number: 75–16636
ISBN: 087013-194-X
MANUFACTURED IN THE UNITED STATES OF AMERICA

★
 ★
★
 ★
 ★

TO

AURELIA AND ROBIN
JIM AND SUE, RICK, CHRISTY
JERRY AND FRAN, NICK
EVAN, MATT

Contents

Introduction

IN 1775 the Continental Congress was summoned to reconvene in Philadelphia. Silas Deane, merchant, member of the Connecticut General Assembly, and one of the three delegates to the Congress from that colony, left his home in Wethersfield to serve the revolutionary cause. The personal cost was to be far greater than he foresaw, for not only would he never see his wife or home again but he would spend the last decade of his life in poverty, illness, and disgrace.

Deane's political enemies would accuse him of betraying the Revolution on three counts: converting a gift into a private commercial transaction; being in private trade while conducting public business; committing treason by writing to friends urging reconciliation with Great Britain. No court of law ever charged Deane with treason, but the court of public opinion indicted and convicted him on circumstantial evidence. For the last two decades of his life Deane sought in vain for "simple justice."

On the first count, Deane has been exonerated. On the second charge, the record shows he was technically guilty of engaging in private commerce while holding a public commission (conflict of interest). On the charge of treason, Deane protested his innocence as long as he lived, maintaining that his letters were to friends and that he, as a citizen, had every right to express his opinions. His contemporaries disagreed.

The accusations against Silas Deane resulted in part from the lack of a well-defined line between public and private interest and from a general distrust of the merchant class. The business code of the eighteenth century prohibited the use of government money or property for private ends. However, so long as the government's interests were not betrayed, the boundary between public and private interest was open, broad, and, in the final analysis, determined by the merchant's conscience. The vagueness of this ethical code was further complicated by the suspicion of many eighteenth-century rural Americans that a man could not be both honorable and a merchant.

The verdict of the revolutionary generation has remained unchanged and largely unchallenged for almost two centuries. Now that the men and passion of the revolutionary period have faded, it is time to review Silas Deane's case. This study is an attempt to grant Silas Deane his day in court with the reader as the unbiased jury.

In the strict sense of the word, no man writes a book entirely by himself, and this volume is no exception. To Dr. Robert Brown, Professor of History of Michigan State University, I am indebted for introducing me to Silas Deane, and to Dr. Robert Ferrell, Professor of History of Indiana University, for his critical advice and sustained interest in America's first diplomatic agent.

It is a privilege to acknowledge the suggestions and criticisms from my colleagues of the Albion College faculty. A special thanks goes to Professor Isolde Henninger, who read and criticized the manuscript in its various stages, either wholly or in part.

To Dr. Edward N. MacConomy, former Head Librarian of Albion College and now in the Library of Congress, and to Elizabeth Hance, Associate Librarian of Albion College, my special thanks for their many services.

CHAPTER 1

HIS EARLY YEARS

THE first foreign agent of the Continental Congress to France, Silas Deane, was born December 24, 1737, to Silas and Sarah Deane of Connecticut. No one prophesied that this son of a blacksmith in an almost unknown village in a remote corner of the world would one day aid in the intrigues of foreign ministers, nor that the fate of the New World might turn on his judgment.

Little is certain of the early life of this future revolutionary leader. He was one of seven children—Barnabas, Barazillai, Silas, Simeon, John, David, and Hannah. David died in infancy, and John at sea in 1778. The surviving brothers became respected merchants in Connecticut. Hannah married Josiah Buck, also a merchant in Connecticut.[1]

The Deanes were not wealthy but possessed sufficient resources to aid their children. After graduating from Yale in 1758, young Silas Deane taught school by day and studied law by night. He was admitted to the bar in 1761 and entered law practice in Wethersfield, one of the colony's thriving commercial river towns.

On October 8, 1763, he married Mehitabel Webb, the widow of a merchant, Joseph Webb. Mehitabel was five years Deane's senior, had five children from her previous marriage, and owned a general store. Deane joined her in business and soon became known as a man of enterprise, vigor, and judgment. He engaged in West Indies trade, and his fortune prospered. Mehitabel Webb had lived in the old Webb house known throughout Connecticut as Hospitality Hall. Silas Deane selected the site next to this and in 1764 built a substantial place which became the family residence. He and Mehitabel had one son, Jesse.

After Mehitabel's death in 1767, and in accord with the colonial custom of early remarriage, Deane promptly took a new wife, Elizabeth Saltonstall, the granddaughter of Gurdon Saltonstall, the former governor of Connecticut. This marriage introduced him to wider social and political circles. The second Mrs. Deane died while Deane was in France on his first mission.

Deane's feelings for his family seem to have been excellent. He was a good provider, and his letters show him to have been affectionate.

A strong lifelong bond of respect existed between Deane and his eldest stepson, Samuel Blachley Webb. When young Webb entered on a commercial enterprise in 1773, Deane wrote a letter of fatherly advice about conducting business affairs in an efficient manner.[2] When Deane went to Congress in 1774 he was "attended" by Samuel B. Webb, and after the Battle of Bunker Hill he secured his eldest stepson a position on Washington's staff. Samuel rose to the rank of a general officer. In June 1778 he told his uncle, Barnabas Deane: "When you write our friend in France [his stepfather] assure him of my warmest affection for him, and the little boy Jesse [his half brother]."[3] His admiration never wavered through later years of Deane's trouble and disgrace.

Although Deane was fond of his numerous family, in later years some of his stepchildren did not hold him in high esteem. His business procedures, or possibly carelessness, appeared a deliberate attempt to defraud them. However, it seems likely that Deane's failure to settle Mehitabel's estate was a result of the unusual circumstances which took him to Europe during the Revolution.

If Samuel B. Webb refused to embarrass Deane by requesting a property settlement of his father's estate, the same cannot be said of John and Joseph Webb or of John Simpson, the husband of their sister, Sarah Webb. As early as March 1775 Simpson was writing Samuel B. Webb: "I think that the conduct of Silas Deane is very extraordinary and derogatory to the character he has always enjoyed."[4] Through the years Joseph Webb showed increasing irritation with Deane's lack of accounting. Deeply involved in revolutionary activities, Deane failed to settle the Webb estate prior to his first mission to France; and, as he never returned to Wethersfield, the estate was not settled in his lifetime.

[2]

But no charge was ever made that Deane had not been a good father. When he married Mehitabel, he had been appointed legal guardian of three of the five Webb children; later he stipulated that all five were to share in his estate equally with his own son, Jesse. To the end, Deane wrote and spoke of the family with great regard and affection.

Whatever Deane's later difficulties with his stepchildren, by the late 1760s he had established himself in law, business, and politics. He had become active in the civic life of Wethersfield and the political life of the colony.

Deane was of medium stature, made a good personal appearance, had striking manners, and had good taste in apparel; he lived in a style worthy of a gentleman of his social position. He was well-educated, possessed an active intellect, and throughout his life revealed in his letters that his correspondents were as many and as varied as the subjects they discussed. He expressed his views with a clarity, force, and frankness that revealed a strong and independent mind.

One of Wethersfield's leading citizens, he entered every phase of community life. In 1768 his friends and neighbors elected him representative in the Colonial Assembly of Connecticut.

He soon became a prominent member of this assembly. Before the trouble with Great Britain demanded his attention, he was appointed by the governor of the colony to a Commission of Five to receive money "to be raised by lottery for erecting buoys and other monuments on the Saybrook Bar."[5] In 1775 the lower house of the assembly also appointed him to serve on a joint committee to consider a letter to the Earl of Dartmouth, the British secretary of state, complaining of the "dissension due to British aggression and the unlimited power claimed by Parliament which were driving the Americans to the border of despair."[6] He was a member of a commission nominated by the Governor's Council and approved by the assembly "to assist Governor Trumbull, in stating and taking proper steps to preserve the claims of this colony to said Western Lands."[7] This commission asserted Connecticut's claims to lands along the Susquehanna River. He earned Governor Jonathan Trumbull's respect for "collecting and preparing all exhibits and documents necessary to pursue and prosecute the claim and title."[8]

Deane had already protested the British laws restricting American com-

[3]

merce when the trouble with Great Britain emerged as the dominant issue of colonial politics. When Connecticut merchants adopted a policy of nonintercourse with British commerce, Deane, acting as their clerk, signed a circular letter of February 10, 1774, accusing the Newport merchants of violating the nonimportation agreement.[9] Similar zeal for the colonial case appeared when Wethersfield residents passed a resolution of sympathy for Boston's suffering caused by closing the port of Boston in retaliation for the Boston Tea Party. A committee was to receive contributions and forward them to Boston; the name of Silas Deane was high on the list. Deane was also Secretary of the Connecticut Committee of Correspondence, and he, Judge Roger Sherman, and Colonel Eliphalet Dyer represented the colony in 1774 at the Congress in Philadelphia.[10]

When he left Wethersfield for Congress in August 1774, Deane was thirty-four years old. Fellow citizens escorted him to Middletown when he departed for Philadelphia. At New Haven his party joined Judge Sherman, and at Fairfield they met Colonel Dyer.

Deane was anxious to meet and judge the temper of his fellow delegates to the Congress. The first night he dined with delegates from Boston and South Carolina, many of whom were also in the mercantile business. "The glass had circulated just long enough to raise the spirits of everyone to that nice point which is above disguise or suspicion," he wrote. "Of consequence, I saw instantly that it was an excellent opportunity to know their real sentiment. Cool myself, I was not afraid of sharing in the jovial entertainment; therefore, after introduction, I wav'd the formality of sitting at the upper part among my brother Delegates, and mixed among the gentlemen of the City." The delegates from Virginia and other southern states pleased him. "They appear," he wrote his wife, "like men of importance—sociable, sensible, and spirited men."[11] As a patriot he spoke of the "prospects of unanimity"; as a politician he noted that "The more I converse in the city, the more I see and lament the virulence of party"; as a statesman he recognized the "arduous task before us." Declaring himself a secessionist, Deane prophesied the greatness of the Congress, which he described as "the grandest and most important assembly ever held in America, . . . all of America is entrusted to it and depends upon it." Deane proclaimed, "The resolutions of the Congress shall be the laws of the Medes and Persians."[12]

Events moved rapidly during the interlude between the Continental Congresses of 1774 and 1775, and Deane occupied himself with the revolutionary cause. To Ebenezer Watson, the editor of the *Connecticut Courant,* he stated his attitude toward independence: "There is no alternative except submit or prepare to resist even unto blood."[13] Before the Congress reassembled in 1775, he added to his reputation as a revolutionist by not only signing a promissory note to help pay for the expedition against Ticonderoga, but sharing in a strategic plan for the undertaking. The Ticonderoga campaign was no act of bravado, but a calculated military move. The cannon captured from Ticonderoga later forced the British to evacuate Boston. For sharing in this success, Silas Deane was nicknamed "Ticonderoga" by his grateful countrymen.

Between sessions of Congress, Deane wrote an agreement signed by one hundred young men who volunteered for the "Lexington Alarm" of 1775, assisting the Provincials at Cambridge. They pledged their services, and vowed to refrain from drunkenness, gaming, and profanity.

As a Connecticut representative in Congress, Deane was proud of his colony and its men who served in the army. When the Wethersfield Rifle Company "appeared with honor on a recent occasion," he wrote, "this has made me an inch taller, though I am prouder, as I may say, of Connecticut than I dare express, not a Colony on the Continent standing in higher estimation among the Colonies."[14]

In the Second Continental Congress Deane engaged in much committee work. The lines of division between revolutionists and loyalists appeared more sharply than before; the determination to resist Great Britain and her policies was by no means unanimous. George Washington, Colonel Philip Schuyler, Deane, and others considered means of procuring military supplies.[15] He helped form rules for the infant navy, and on October 15, 1775, selected and purchased the first vessel.[16] Deane served with Washington on another committee to draft rules for the army.[17] With John Adams and Benjamin Franklin he made an inquiry during a recess of Congress about virgin lead and leaden ore and the means of refining the mineral, obviously of importance for the prosecution of war.[18]

His mercantile experience gave Deane the background for discussing the commercial policies considered by the Congress. When the "State of Trade" was debated, he declared: "I think all Colonies ought to have free and equal footing; we must have trade. I think we ought to apply abroad, we must

[5]

have powder and goods; we can't keep our people easy without it."[19] He favored opening American ports to foreign ships, a practice not permitted under the English Navigation Acts.

His experience in Congress gave Deane confidence in his abilities. His committee assignments were many and varied; the work, arduous and time consuming. He described a typical day to his wife: "I rise at six, write until seven, dress and breakfast by eight, go to the Committee on Claims until ten; then in Congress till half past three or perhaps four; dine by five, and then go either to the Committee of Secrecy, or of Trade until nine; then sup and go to bed by eleven. This leaves little time for diversion or anything else, and to tell you the truth I expect this kind of life may be my lot for some time to come." He summed up his attitude toward his activities explaining that even a ride in the countryside was to discuss "Another bold stroke like that of Ticonderoga." He admitted that his constant preoccupation with plans and schemes had unhappily and erroneously caused his colleagues and others to think of him as a "schemer," and that it had brought him more than his share of business both in and out of Committee. Sadly, he concluded that anyone in public life greatly reduced his chances for happiness.[20]

In spite of Deane's preoccupation with congressional affairs, he sent frequent political reports to Connecticut Governor Trumbull and other political friends. In letters to his wife he discussed men and events freely and frankly. Her health was of particular concern, and the general welfare of the family was never forgotten. Numerous references were made to Sarah [Sally], John, and other family members.

Illness prevented Mrs. Deane from joining her husband in Philadelphia, but it did not lessen her interest in the social life of the new capital city. Occasionally she chided him for his failure to describe the ladies and the fashions of the day, but he reminded her that she was aware that he was most indifferent in ladies' company, although he did visit the drawing rooms of Philadelphia and engaged in light conversation "merely to chase away the spleen."

Since the outbreak of the quarrel between Great Britain and her colonies, Deane had served the colonial cause without regard to his personal comfort or cost. In July and September 1774 he wrote his wife of his devotion to the cause of liberty and his willingness to serve the revolutionary cause in any capacity. Perhaps with a tinge of self-righteousness, he wrote that his principles were to sacrifice all lesser considerations to the service of the whole and cheerfully sacrifice private fortune, comfort, "even my life to save the jewel of Liberty. This being my line of conduct, I have a calmness of mind . . . which more than balances every external trouble: of which I have not a few."

By the fall of 1774 he had reached the conclusion that "Liberty or Death is before us, and I can conceive of no alternative. . . ." In October he wrote, "I am enlisted in the general service, and must take my post, if possible, where I have a chance of doing most service."[21] Deane's principles were put to the acid test when in October 1775 the Connecticut Assembly refused to nominate him for a third year. Hurt, and feeling that his recall was a censure of his conduct, Deane considered returning to Connecticut and demanding a public investigation. However, to his wife he merely wrote that "I am quite willing to quit my station to abler men; and who they are, the Colony knows, or ought to know, best."[22]

From Connecticut he received conflicting reports. Thomas Mumford, a Connecticut friend of long standing, intimated to Deane that there were false as well as true friends in the General Assembly of Connecticut. John Trumbull, brother of the Connecticut governor and another close friend, in a long philosophical letter attributed Deane's recall to the malice and envy of free people: "I doubt not you will be able to survive all their malice and envy, tho' you know we have a strange people here as elsewhere." He continued, "it is dangerous, they say . . . to trust so great a power as you now have for a long time in the hands of one set of men, least they grow too self-important, and cause a great deal of mischief in the end."[23]

Prominent in congressional affairs, "reckoned a good man, and much esteemed in Congress,"[24] Deane seems not to have aroused the resentment of any sectional or interest group represented in Congress. Later, in 1778 when the Deane-Lee feud was at its height, Samuel Adams was the only member to recall a suspicion of Silas Deane.[25] Deane's failure to secure reappointment was the result of his neglect of local politics for national affairs. His support for some "favorite sons" and opposition to others seeking Continental appointments had caused wide resentment in the Connecticut Assembly. His failure to support fully some of the Connecticut Accounts against Congress had also aroused some ill will. Relations between Sherman, Dyer, and Deane had been correct if not friendly.

Revolutionary events began to move rapidly. Throughout 1774 and 1775 Englishmen in America had sought to find a formula to reconcile colonial and imperial differences on legal grounds, with only a small minority advocating resistance by force. In April at Lexington and Concord and in June 1775 at Bunker Hill blood had been shed, but pride in British citizenship sustained the desire for reconciliation.

The issues of liberty and independence were joined in August 1775 when a Royal Proclamation declared the "Uprisings" in the colonies "Rebellion" and the participants "Traitors." On December 22, again by Royal Proclamation, American goods were declared contraband and intercourse with the rebels was forbidden. Insult was added to injury when Hessian mercenaries were hired to subdue the rebels.

Despite failing to be re-elected, Deane continued to serve the revolutionary cause unofficially. One of the last acts of the naval committee of the Second Continental Congress was to direct Deane to go to New York to buy a ship to carry twenty nine-pounders and a sloop of ten guns, fit them out, and send them through the Sound to New London for seamen and arms. Deane reported to his wife that "Colonel Dyer plead, scolded, fretted, and even threatened me, to make me set out for home with him," but Deane decided to remain and help with the naval preparation. He had, as he put it, selected his line of conduct.[26]

Richard Henry Lee of Virginia introduced the famous Resolution for Independence on June 6, 1776. Lee recommended working toward independence, foreign aid and alliances, and opening the ports to foreign—that is, non-British—commerce. To declare for independence would disrupt ancient loyalties. The decision to seek foreign aid was equally agonizing. Some individuals thought such moves would destroy any hope of reconciliation; others thought them disgraceful; a small minority felt the steps unnecessary. It took time and debate to appoint a committee of five "for the sole purpose of corresponding with our friends in Great Britain, Ireland, and other parts of the world."[27] Eventually this committee was composed of Benjamin Franklin, Benjamin Harrison, Thomas Johnson, John Dickinson, and John

Jay. Two months later the committee added Robert Morris. Known at first as the Committee of Correspondence, then as the Committee of Secret Correspondence, Congress on April 17, 1777, resolved that "for the future, it be styled the Committee for Foreign Affairs." Here was the precursor of the Department of State.

To probe foreign sentiment and obtain information useful in the revolutionary struggle, the Committee took a step toward foreign aid on December 13, 1775, requesting Arthur Lee in London to learn the disposition of foreign powers toward the Americans. It warned of the need for "great circumspection and impenetrable secrecy."[28]

The country to which Congress naturally looked was Great Britain's established rival, France, who had, in fact, initiated an early informal approach. Through a French citizen, Achard de Bonvouloir, "a traveler out of curiosity" who denied he had official status, the Committee learned that the French Government would not put obstacles in the way of supplies. Early in January 1776, two Frenchmen, Penet and Pliarne, who had approached General Washington, appeared in Philadelphia and negotiated to supply munitions and goods.

The time had come to approach France directly; the man selected for this delicate task was Silas Deane, the "lame duck" from Connecticut. He had worked on many other assignments with the Committee of Secret Correspondence and knew the needs of his country, especially those of the nascent army and navy. He was willing to go and accepted the commission.

Deane was aware of the difficulties. His family needed his attention. He had been away from home a long time; his wife was in poor health, his son Jesse at a tender age. In a letter to his wife he admitted he was needed at home:

I can but feel for the pain I must give you by this adventure, but on all occasions you will have this satisfaction, that let what will happen, you have in every situation discharged your duty as one of the best of partners and wives, while on my part, by a peculiar fatality attending me from my first entrance into public life, I have ever been involved in one scheme and adventure after another, so as to keep my mind in constant agitation and my attention fixed on other objects than my own immediate interests.[29]

[9]

The Commerce Committee authorized Deane to export from France certain articles suitable for the Indians and instructed him as to the quality of the merchandise he was to buy. He would receive a commission of five percent on remittances to Europe. The United Colonies were to bear the full cost, including insurance and risk of capture at sea. The Committee signed the agreement.[30]

At the same time the Committee of Secret Correspondence also commissioned Deane to "go to France, there to transact such Business, commercial and political, as we have committed to his Care, in Behalf and by Authority of the Congress of the Thirteen United Colonies."[31]

No comment or criticism of Deane's appointment and departure to France as an agent of the Committee was voiced in or out of Congress. In fact, his appointment was kept secret from the main body of Congress, but when the fact leaked out several months later, intense personal jealousies added their bitterness to the already growing division in Congress between the agricultural and commercial interests of the nation and those who still questioned the need and desirability of securing foreign aid.

Before leaving, Deane obtained contracts, instructions, letters of introduction, and a "Character Testimonial" signed by all the members in town except Bartlett of New Hampshire, the Adamses and Ward." He wrote his wife: "And now, my Dear, are not the ways of Providence dark and inscrutable to us, short-sighted mortals? Surely they are. My enemies tho't to triumph over me and bring me down, yet all they did has been turned to the opening a door for the greatest and most extensive usefulness, if I succeed; but if I fail,—why then the Cause I am engaged in, and the important part I have undertaken, will justify my adventuring."[32]

One big question remains on Deane's selection: had the Committee of Correspondence chosen the most appropriate or talented man for Congress's first delicate foreign assignment?

CHAPTER 2

AS AGENT OF THE SECRET
COMMITTEE OF CORRESPONDENCE

DEANE'S decision to head a one-man mission to France opened a new phase of the American Revolution, as well as a new chapter in his life. While serving on committees as a member of Congress, he had acquired knowledge of the army and navy. Successful in the commercial world, he could wear an authentic guise as a colonial merchant abroad. His reason for accepting was a sense of duty and desire to serve his country, for assuming the post entailed personal sacrifice. As Deane at the moment was financially independent, promise of the five percent commission was not enticing. Separation from his wife and child was a source of anguish, and sea voyages were seldom pleasant. To the unpleasantness of the voyage he had to add the danger of capture by the British, which could mean internment or possibly death.

Deane's mission to France falls into two parts. During the first phase, from July 1776 until December 1776, he was the sole representative of the Committee of Secret Correspondence in France, serving both as a diplomatic and commercial agent. From December 1776 until his recall, Deane worked with Benjamin Franklin and Arthur Lee; this three-man commission was authorized by Congress to negotiate an alliance with France.

Deane received his instructions from the Secret Committee of Correspondence in a letter written by Benjamin Franklin on March 3, 1776. Posing as a merchant buying goods for the American Indian trade, he was ordered to: secure supplies from the French government and promote an alliance with France; contact C. W. F. Dumas, the colonial agent in Holland; correspond with Dr. Edward Bancroft of London; and remain in touch with Arthur Lee, the colonial agent in London. In addition, he was to defend the colonies against "calumnies."[1] To reduce the danger of being captured by a British man-of-war, he was to go to France by way of Bermuda and Spain.

He sailed in March 1776. Landing in Spain, he made his way over the Pyrenees, reaching France in July. Before going to Paris, he stopped in Bordeaux and purchased supplies for the Indian trade. His cover as a merchant abroad did not deceive British intelligence, but the reports to London underrated him and misrepresented his reception by the French government.

Paris introduced him to a new way of life. At first he stayed in ordinary hotels and attempted to make himself inconspicuous by frequently changing his lodging. His frugal manner of living was dictated partly by the failure of Congress to send credit and American merchandise to cover his bills, partly by his determination to remain inconspicuous. He depicted himself to C. W. F. Dumas as a private gentleman, "as such I am in Paris, and that character I shall keep unless . . . obliged to alter it. Parade and pomp have no charms in the eyes of a patriot, or even a man of common sense; but at the same time, I can never submit to the changing of my name, unless I am convinced that so humiliating a step will promote the service of my country."[2] Throughout the first part of his mission—before Franklin and Lee arrived—Deane was never free from financial worries. Of this there is abundant evidence in his private correspondence and reports to the Committee of Secret Correspondence. On August 18, 1776, he wrote the Committee: "I must again remind you of my situation here. The bills designed for my use are protested, and expenses rising fast in consequence of the business of my hands, which I may on no account neglect, and a small douceur, though I have been sparing in that way, is sometimes of the utmost importance. The quantity of stores to be shipped will amount to a large sum; the very charge of them will be great, for which I am the only responsible person."[3]

There were other special embarrassments with which Deane entered upon his mission. He did not speak French nor know the customs of the land, and he was ignorant of court etiquette. His instructions warned that the court might not like it known that an agent of the colonies was in the country. Deane was told that Monsieur le Roy at the Louvre and Monsieur Barbeu du Bourg would introduce him to the friends of America.[4] For a "merchant of Connecticut" to be received by French ministers was more than he dared expect.

Deane was conscious of being surrounded by enemies. These were, of course, the British agents. He also knew every word uttered would be reported to the French ministers. "My arrival here, my name, my lodging, and many other particulars have been reported to the British administration . . . the city swarms with Englishmen, and as money purchases everything in this country, I have had, and still have, a most difficult task to avoid their machinations. Not a coffee house or theater or other place of public diversion but swarms with their emissaries . . ."[5] To prevent incidents he determined to avoid meeting any English-speaking people in public. This action caused Beaumarchais to remark that if M. Deane did not "open his mouth before the English speaking people he meets; . . . he must be the most silent man in Paris, for I defy him to say six consecutive words" in French.[6]

Nevertheless, he was warmly received by the "friends of America." He immediately presented his letter of introduction to Du Bourg, an influential scientist and long-time friend of Benjamin Franklin.

Upon Deane's insistence, Du Bourg arranged for a secret meeting with the minister of foreign affairs, the Comte de Vergennes. During the two-hour interview conducted through an interpreter, Vergennes sought to learn about the colonies, and Deane attempted to discover the possibilities of French aid and the probable European reception of the contemplated Declaration of Independence. Vergennes carefully pointed out that any open aid by France could disturb relations with Great Britain. At the same time he assured Deane that the latter, as a private citizen, was free to carry on commerce in the kingdom. The minister remarked that the French army had recently adopted new weapons and that the old models remained in the arsenals. Deane should consider himself under the protection of the French court, and though he would not be officially recognized he could always reach Vergennes through Gérard, head of the political section of the Foreign Office. As the interview ended, Vergennes assured Deane that "The people and their cause are very respectable in the eyes of all disinterested persons . . ."[7]

Deane was pleased, not knowing, of course, that France had been preparing for such an agent since 1763. The then minister of foreign affairs, the Duc de Choiseul, "scarcely before the ink was dry on the pen" which had signed the Treaty of Paris with Great Britain, had originated a policy of preparing for a new Anglo-French struggle.[8] The files of the French Foreign Office contained maps of the English coast with designated landing areas; the French military forces, army and navy, had been enlarged. Through the years French agents had reported the temper of Englishmen in North America. Perhaps the time had now come to reopen the struggle.

The French government carefully consulted its own interests before openly aiding the American colonies. In 1776 a form of despotism ruled France. The government was nominally under the king's sole control, but whereas Louis XIV had dominated his ministers, Louis XVI was controlled by them. The latter wished to serve France and considered its interests primary. He had no great love for the revolting colonies, but in the end was unable or unwilling to resist the pro-American views of his three chief advisers: the Comte de Maurepas, the principal adviser and an astute political observer; Antoine de Sartine, the Minister of Marine, an able administrator; and Vergennes, the Minister of Foreign Affairs, heir to Choiseul's policy of revenge toward Great Britain and the "strong man of the government." Turgot, the Controller of the Treasury, opposed war because of the strain it would place on the French treasury. Turgot might have influenced Louis XVI, but his resignation in May 1776 removed a barrier to the pro-American policy. French intervention became a question only of how and when. The "when" forced a policy of watchful waiting; the decision was not made until 1777 when Vergennes felt that the tide of war in North America had turned in favor of the Americans. As for the "how," it was supplied for the delicate time being by a most extraordinary person, Pierre Augustin Caron de Beaumarchais.

The relations between Vergennes and Beaumarchais are a study in contrasting personalities working for a common goal. In 1776 Vergennes was fifty-four years old. From his youth he had trained himself for diplomacy, and served apprenticeship in the principal courts of Europe. Grave, laborious, methodical, he could keep his own counsel until the time for action.

He wished the Americans well if only to humble Great Britain, but was determined to take no step that would embarrass France without realizing French objectives. His political morals were no worse than those of the average diplomat of his day. That he deceived Lord Stormont, the British ambassador, was a legitimate part of his statecraft. He was not above employing spies among his friends. It is questionable whether much transpired which he did not know. He left office a man of moderate means, which suggests his honesty in state finance, a rare quality in the eighteenth century.

If Vergennes was deliberate by nature and training, the same cannot be said for the flamboyant Beaumarchais, whose pro-American views were well known. An early convert to the American cause, Beaumarchais had been a self-styled "watchmaker of the King", unsalaried music teacher of the king's daughters, controller of the pantry, the king's secretary (by right of purchase), author of the popular *Le Mariage de Figaro,* husband of a rich widow, a man trusted by two kings on missions so delicate they could not be handled through diplomatic channels.

In London on a "delicate mission" in 1775, this adventurer saw Arthur Lee, the agent in Great Britain of the Secret Committee of Correspondence. The two men met at the home of John Wilkes, the well-known English radical. Beaumarchais, although not authorized to commit the French government to a sou, perhaps from enthusiasm may have promised five million livres of arms and ammunition for the American cause. When he returned to Paris, he did launch a crusade for French support for the Americans. He bombarded Vergennes and the king with memorials to support the rebels. His suggestions included a plan whereby the French government could aid the Americans through a private corporation using official funds.[9]

Vergennes calculated the risk involved. For some time the foreign minister had been reviewing Anglo-French relations and explaining to Louis XVI and his colleagues the advantages to France of aiding the colonies. He decided in favor of secret aid, the postponement of active intervention pending future military developments.

British military victories in the rebellious colonies were the decisive factor in Vergennes's decision to limit France's participation to secret aid. However, the failure of Congress to formally declare independence presented a legal problem for the French foreign minister. Vergennes, trained in the legalistic school of diplomacy, was too prudent to make a premature show of interest, because "neither the dignity of the King, nor his interests, permitted him to enter into a pact with the Insurgents. . . . Such a pact, in truth, would be worthless until they had rendered themselves independent and shown a disposition to remain firm."

On August 10, 1776, the day it arrived in London, the Declaration of Independence was published in the *London Gazette*. Three days later, after the publication of the news in Great Britain, M. Garnier, the French Charge d'Affaires in London, wrote his minister that the general reaction in England to the American Declaration of Independence was negative. On August 16 Garnier equated the Declaration of Independence with a declaration of war by Congress. Unfortunately for Silas Deane, after the Declaration reached London more than three months passed before official notification reached the court of France. It appeared to both Vergennes and Deane that Congress had decided not to seek French aid, and that the Secret Committee had forgotten they had an agent in Paris.

For Deane it was a time of perplexity, inexpressible anxiety, and embarrassment. All the newspapers of Europe were publishing the text of the Declaration, and freely commenting thereon; he alone was without information. If he had been a seasoned ambassador, he could not have done better in defending the American interest. He constantly reiterated his unshakable faith in the determination of Congress to persevere to the end. He continually reminded the minister of the causes that could account for the silence of Congress—the treachery of the sea, the danger of capture, the fortunes of war, and congressional preoccupation with daily survival.

The Declaration of Independence was unanimously adopted by Congress on July 4, and it was ordered that it should be proclaimed in each of the United States and read to the army. That was all. It does not appear that anyone thought it appropriate to send copies to the several courts of Europe whose friendship the Congress was already trying to conciliate. Congress not only failed to exploit the propaganda value of the Declaration; it also unintentionally almost ruined the opportunity to secure the French alliance.

The time required to transmit a message to Europe varied from thirty days to three months, depending upon the winds and the season. On July

8 the Secret Committee sent instructions to Deane in Paris to "make the act known to the Court of France and the other powers of Europe" with a printed copy of the Declaration. The vessel was never heard from. A month later the Committee sent a duplicate copy with the same instructions. The second ship sailed August 7, and thirty-eight days later reached the coast of France. The Declaration was delivered to Silas Deane on November 17. The captain of the vessel had forgotten to deliver the packet.

On November 20, 1776, the formal presentation took place. Although Vergennes's objections had been removed, the military situation in America forced Vergennes to conclude that it was an inopportune time for France to openly espouse the American cause. Officially rebuffed, Deane was forced to turn to unofficial sources for the supplies so desperately needed by the American army.[10]

Deane had confederates in high French circles. One of the factors that determined his selection by the Secret Committee of Correspondence for the mission to France was his knowledge of the needs of the American army. In his first interview with Vergennes he learned that the French army had been newly equipped and he obtained permission to engage in trade. Vergennes was thoughtful enough to suggest that Deane communicate with Beaumarchais. When questioned about Beaumarchais's financial standing, Vergennes assured Deane that Beaumarchais was capable of fulfilling a large contract.[11] Deane called on Beaumarchais; and when Beaumarchais as head of Rodrigue Hortalez and Company offered to ship three million livres of goods on the credit of Congress, Deane accepted.

The American representative in Paris was confused. Rumors were rife in Paris that Beaumarchais's financial standing was dubious. In gratitude for the promised help, but with some bewilderment, Deane wrote in August to the Secret Committee of Correspondence "that a man should but a few months since confine himself from his creditors, and now on this occasion be able to advance half a million, is so extraordinary that it ceases to be a mystery." Deane explained, "everything he says, writes or does, is in reality the action of the ministry."[12] By December he was referring to Beaumarchais as "my minister." Deane's fear and anxiety for the quality of the supplies was revealed in a letter to John Jay. Deane warned that the goods should be carefully inspected upon arrival. He admitted that he did not think it wise to insist upon a careful inspection because they were from "persons in such station that had I hesitated it might have ruined my affairs."[13]

With such common purpose the terms of a contract were soon agreed upon and the collection and forwarding of supplies to America began. According to the contract, Beaumarchais was to procure supplies, to be paid for by tobacco and other articles as fast as vessels could be provided.[14] Deane asked no longer credit than twelve months and hoped remittance would be within six months.[15] Beaumarchais requested lists of supplies, and apologized that his resources were not as large as desired. He stated that it would be necessary to have prompt returns to continue his advances. He assured Deane: "I desire to serve your country as if it were my own, and I hope to find the friendship of a generous people the true reward of a labor that I consecrate to them."[16]

The contract clearly stated that the supplies were to be paid for and were not a gift. The Committee, in instructing Deane to obtain clothing and arms for twenty-five thousand men, had said: "We mean to pay for the same by remittances . . ." Linens, woolens, and other merchandise were to be settled at once on a cash basis.[17] Deane informed the Committee he was negotiating with Beaumarchais on the basis of eight months' credit from time of delivery, and that he had certified to the French merchants "that Congress would pay for whatever stores they would credit them with." He warned Congress: "If I effect this, as I undoubtedly shall, I must rely on the remittances being made this fall and winter without fail, or the credit of the colonies must suffer."[18] Beaumarchais as head of Rodrigue Hortalez and Company was also explicit when he reported on the transaction to the Secret Committee: "I request of you, gentlemen, to send me next Spring, if it is possible for you, ten or twelve thousand hogsheads, or more, if you can, of tobacco from Virginia, of the best quality."[19]

Unfortunately, difficulties occurred. The Secret Committee of Correspondence never once replied to Rodrigue Hortalez's many letters. Perhaps Congress wondered why supplies continued to arrive without payment. Neither Deane nor Beaumarchais realized that Arthur Lee, with whom Beaumarchais had discussed the sending of military supplies, was frantically writing from England to his brothers and Congress that the French government did not expect any pay, that Beaumarchais was not a merchant, and that he, Lee, felt that what had been a gift had become a commercial transaction—for the benefit of Deane and Beaumarchais at the expense of Congress.[20]

Having made a contract, Beaumarchais executed it with zest and spirit. He rented the Hôtel de Hollande, once the residence of the Dutch ambassador, and there with a great force of clerks disproved Du Bourg's assertion that in France people would hesitate to do business with him.[21] For as the playwright-turned-merchant wrote Congress, "I dare promise to you, gentlemen, that my indefatigable zeal shall never be wanting to clear up difficulties, soften prohibition, and, in short, facilitate all operations of a commerce which my advantage, much less than yours, has made me undertake with you."[22]

The selection, collection, and shipping of arms and munitions to ports of France from the royal arsenals constitute an amazing story. In spite of France's official neutrality, Beaumarchais's men avoided detection by British agents and at the same time cut French bureaucratic red tape. To be sure, there was unofficial help from the French government.

When Vergennes indicated to Deane that it might be possible to receive military supplies from France, the minister did not say or intimate that he had anticipated such a request. The truth is that in 1775 the French minister of war, St. Germain, had ordered an eminent French artillery officer, Du Coudray, to visit the arsenals to determine what munitions could be drawn for American purposes. Early in September 1776, Du Coudray visited Strasbourg, Dijon, Metz, Besançon, and Charterville, where he selected "two hundred four pounder field pieces, a hundred thousand balls, twenty-five thousand small arms with ammunition, and tents for twenty-five thousand men."[23] Such preparations permitted greater expediency. Under cover of darkness, almost literally under the noses of British intelligence, the supplies moved to the coast. When Deane informed Beaumarchais he could not provide American vessels, the Frenchman supplied ships and went in person to supervise their loading.

Beaumarchais was tireless, but not always judicious. When he went to Le Havre to supervise the cargoes, he took the name of Durant, but as one of his comedies was playing the city he did not hesitate to attend rehearsals and coach the actors. His presence became known to British agents; his assumed name became meaningless. Through Stormont, the British government protested. The evidence was so irrefutable that Vergennes was forced to issue a restraining order. Before the government ordered the operation to cease, however, the first vessel carrying munitions and cannons, the *Amphitrite,* sailed on December 14, 1776, from Le Havre. Events caused it to return to port a few days later, much to the disgust of Deane and Beaumarchais, but other vessels were almost ready to leave, and Beaumarchais gave Vergennes no rest until the government lifted the ban and the ships sailed.

Eight shiploads of supplies were sent to the colonies, with only one (the *Seine*) falling into the hands of the British. The *Amphitrite, Mercury, Amelie, Therese, La Mere Bobi, Marie Catherine, and Le Flamand* reached American ports. Including the cost of shipping, the cargoes represented 6,274,844 livres tournois. These supplies, and these alone, made possible the American campaign that resulted in Burgoyne's surrender at Saratoga. To Silas Deane and Beaumarchais belong much of the credit for the successful campaign which brought France into the Revolution as an ally.[24]

So with the approval or at least the connivance of the French government, secret aid reached America. But neither Deane nor Beaumarchais received tobacco or instructions. Beaumarchais could write: "There is no news from America, and no tobacco either. This is depressing, but depression is a long way from discouragement."[25] It was a period of great anxiety for Deane. Through his letters to the Secret Committee of Correspondence ran the melancholy phrases, "without intelligence" and "I am frantic with doubt and despair."[26] In December 1776 he wrote his friend, John Jay: "If my letters arrive safe, they will give you some idea of my situation, without intelligence, without orders, and without remittances, yet boldly plunging into contracts, engagements, and negotiations, hourly hoping that something will arrive from America."[27] But not until January 11, 1777, did Deane learn from Robert Morris, a member of the Secret Committee of Correspondence and often the Committee's secretary, that "I have long been aware that you wou'd suffer vexation from want of remittances . . . yet such has been our situation and circumstances it was not possible to mend the matter."[28]

Meanwhile, Deane unwittingly compromised the secrecy of his work. When he arrived in Europe he did not know a single person. Soon he had widened his friendships. He quickly met Beaumarchais, Du Bourg, and

Vergennes. Unfortunately, his instructions ordered him to write to Dr. Edward Bancroft, an American living in London and a former student of Deane's in Connecticut. Bancroft supposedly had means of supplying political and commercial information. After a short time Bancroft came to Paris at Deane's expense and there learned all the details of Deane's mission. Upon returning to London, Bancroft made a deal with the British government. For five hundred pounds down and four hundred pounds per annum, "Dr. Edwards" (Bancroft) corresponded with a British agent, Paul Wentworth, and communicated whatever came to his knowledge about Deane's letters, the progress of treaties, and commercial or political news.[29] Bancroft served as Deane's confidential adviser and later with Franklin as "semi-secretary of Legation" at Passy. At all times he had access to private papers belonging to the Commission and was even trusted with a key to them.[30] Neither Deane nor Franklin ever suspected his double role.

Bancroft was a curious character. In addition to his political activities and scientific studies, he was a dabbler in stocks. Because of his financial operations he never had the full trust of the British ministers or, especially, of George III. Deane and Franklin both trusted him, defended him against charges by Arthur Lee, and praised him to the Secret Committee of Correspondence and Congress.[31] Bancroft appeared to be genuinely fond of Deane, a fact later demonstrated by the affection and care he showed Deane when the revolutionary envoy was ill and in disgrace in London.

Shortly after Deane's arrival in France, William Carmichael of Maryland stopped in Paris on his way home after an extended visit in England. He met Deane and decided to stay as his aide without pay. Carmichael was of much help, serving as troubleshooter and chief inspector of goods and ships. No evidence supports the later charges by Arthur or William Lee questioning Carmichael's loyalty. That Carmichael was vain and a braggart with great personal charm and some ability cannot be denied. The General Post Office in London regularly intercepted his letters to various lady intimates in England, and the missives provided spicy reading for the censors.

Deane accepted at face value Carmichael's frequent declarations that his only desire was to serve his country and have a little fun, and praised his services to Congress.[32] Later, Carmichael was to give Congress his "understanding" of what he thought was a private commercial transaction. This report was derogatory to Deane. One of Carmichael's great faults, resulting from his arrogance and egotism, was that he felt he should direct the operation. John Jay, on a mission to Spain, discovered that Carmichael as his secretary had to have the center of the stage or his interest wandered. Within six months after arriving in France, Carmichael became critical of Deane and Franklin and disgusted with the French. "I must repeat again," a British agent reported to London, quoting Carmichael, "that Mr. Deane is too open in his transactions and exposes many things that might be kept secret, and swears by all that is sacred that they shall not have anything from him again."[33] The same agent reported that Carmichael was enraged with the French. According to the report, he declared that the French could not be depended upon and if he had the management of affairs the French government would not have the least idea of what was involved in the Commission's transactions.

The American, George Lupton, the paid agent of the British government and a Paris acquaintance of Deane, reported directly to William Eden, the Under-Secretary of State for Foreign Affairs. Lupton posed as an American businessman waiting for capital to invest in American trade. Deane liked and trusted him and they spent a great deal of time together. Lupton reported on Deane's breakfast conversations with Dr. Bancroft and Carmichael.[34] He described Carmichael's trips to Nantes, Bordeaux, and Dunkirk to inspect goods and ships dispatched to America.[35] He discovered and reported that Deane received mail from England via Holland under the name of Monjeui Benson.[36] Once when Deane left the room, Lupton slipped into his closet and read letters and an unfinished dispatch to Congress.[37] He reported that he had met John Nicholson, the captain of a Continental ship, closely associated with Deane in privateering and highly esteemed by him: "I say I got on the blind side of him [Nicholson] and discovered just what I wished for a man of his turn."[38] Lupton was in no way associated with Deane except as a well-wisher, and how long he would have been able to continue the deception will never be known, for the British dropped him from their list of agents in France.

The Secret Committee of Correspondence had instructed Deane to contact Bancroft in London, and they also suggested relations with Arthur Lee in London and with C. W. F. Dumas, the Committee's agent in Holland. Bancroft proved a traitor, and Lee became Deane's worst enemy. But the correspondence with Dumas ripened into a lifelong friendship.

[22]

In his letters to Dumas, Deane clearly expressed his views on affairs of the day. Deane declared his willingness, even eagerness, to assume public responsibilities. "I ever keep in mind the motto, 'de republica nil desperandum,' " he wrote. "I counted the costs when I entered the list, and balanced private fortune, ease, leisure, the sweets of domestic society, and life itself in vain against the liberties of my country; the latter instantly predominated, and I have nothing to complain of, though much to grieve at, occasioned by the miscarriage or delay of my full power for open and public application."[39] As a staunch patriot with a vision of the future, Deane predicted that America would triumph and would become an asylum for "the sons of men in future ages" with "unprecedented laws, liberty, and commerce." Regardless of disappointments, he would never "despair of my country, for which I shall count it my glory to suffer all things, if it receive any advantage therefrom, . . ."[40]

Deane told Dumas that the United States needed foreign aid; he urged Congress to press for an alliance with France. As a merchant, Deane believed in and prophesied the commercial expansion of the British North American colonies in the future. He understood the mercantile systems in Europe. Like John Adams and Franklin, he feared alliances and would have preferred his country to be free of political entanglements, but he was eager for commerce. He wrote: "The United Colonies only ask for what nature surely entitles all men to, a free and uninterrupted commerce and exchange of the superfluities of one country for those of another. . ." He wished the colonies to be free, but did not feel they could gain independence without foreign intervention.[41]

No one could ignore the possibility of a reconciliation with Great Britain. For all Americans abroad this factor made negotiations unsure and difficult. Deane felt it an unnecessary apprehension, and wrote that he had "long been convinced that no act is too atrocious for them [the British] to attempt, nor any report too ridiculous and improbable for them to propagate to serve their purposes." He admitted reconciliation possible, but stated he would not be surprised if Congress decided to continue the war unsupported. "I, who know my countrymen perfectly well, and the principles by which they are actuated, do not believe that they will ever accommodate on terms lower than independence; yet in the same situation, and with the same offers made them, I am certain any other people in the world would accom-

[23]

modate . . ."[42] This conviction did not derive from vanity. While denying any wish to place his countrymen above other nations, he pointed out that the Americans were a people possessing new or at least long unpracticed ideas. It would be difficult to compare them to other nations. That Americans had defied Great Britain was a distinction, an independent act demonstrating worthiness of full independence.

In letters to Dumas, Deane did not hesitate to point out that England had been an exponent of the balance of power; and, that while most politicians and statesmen of Europe thought along these lines, he, Deane, saw a new universal monarchy on the horizon. He prophesied that, if Great Britain had the foresight to form an alliance with the United States and the courage to replace the East India Company when its charter expired in 1780 and the wisdom to maintain her strict and close alliance with Russia, "Great Britain, America, and Russia united will command not barely Europe, but the whole world united."[43]

While Deane philosophized, world events moved forward. By late 1776 the American Revolution was producing mixed reactions in France, but the dominant one was favorable to the colonies. The French government was interested because of the Revolution's effect on Great Britain's colonial and commercial power. French intellectuals were intrigued and hopeful— America represented an experiment along lines indicated by the eighteenth-century political philosophers, the Encyclopedists, Rousseau, and Voltaire.

To professional soldiers the Revolution offered a special opportunity for glory and promotion; their problems took up much of Deane's time. Beaumarchais, admitting that Arthur Lee had first mentioned it to him, suggested a plan for sending officers to America.[44] Deane was aware of the shortage of trained officers. He was conscious that the French War Ministry was forced, as a matter of expediency, to frown upon sending French officers, but that in the final analysis officers were "recommended by the ministry here, and at this instant are really in their army, but this must be kept a secret."[45] The pressure to accept the service of officers was almost unbearable. Early in December 1776 many of them approached Deane to offer their services. He reported their requests to the Secret Committee of Correspondence and asked for instructions. When the Committee failed to respond, he decided to follow Beaumarchais's plan and advice.

Deane's wholesale grant of commissions to foreign officers early in the war became a source of much discontent, and a mixed advantage to the colonists. According to reports of British intelligence, over four hundred French officers served in the American army. Some officers were good, some bad; all occasioned problems. Officers of the Continental Army resented the foreigners.

A contract which caused Congress embarrassment and Deane the most grief was the one from which he had expected the American army to derive the greatest benefit, that of the French artillery officer, Du Coudray. To the Secret Committee of Correspondence, Deane had reported that ministers of the French court had recommended Du Coudray to him as an experienced artillery officer. Deane admitted the offer too "tempting an object for me to hesitate about, though I owe there is a silence in instructions."[46] Despite his good recommendations, Du Coudray managed to displease Deane and Beaumarchais before he sailed for America on December 14, 1776, just in time to avoid the restraining order issued by the French government. In a few days the ship returned because General du Coudray had not liked either his quarters or provisions. Securing a new clearance caused Deane and Beaumarchais much inconvenience and worry. When the ship again sailed, the temperamental Du Coudray had arranged both cargo and passenger list to his satisfaction. Du Coudray and his party reached Philadelphia in June 1777. When he applied for the rank of major general, assigned to him by Deane, with command of the Continental engineers and artillery, the reaction was immediate and violent. Generals Nathanael Greene, Henry Knox, and John Sullivan tendered resignations. Congress did not accept them, but offered Du Coudray the title of Inspector-General of Ordinance, which he agreed to accept. On the eve of the Battle of Brandywine, Du Coudray requested and Congress granted permission for him to join the army as a captain of engineers. He neatly ended his importunities when he drowned while crossing the Schuylkill on September 16, 1777.

Then there was the embarrassing case of the French officer who did not come to America, the Comte de Broglie. An intermediary had suggested to Deane that "Congress should ask of the King of France someone who would become their civil and military chief, the temporary generalissimo of the new republic."[47] Of course, the designated "chief" was to be De Broglie. Deane listened uncertainly. After consulting Benjamin Franklin, in France at that time, he transmitted the request to the Secret Committee of Correspondence. Relaying the request to the Committee, he named the wrong man, which indicates some lack of interest in the affair. Franklin's thoughts and comments are unknown. All parties were saved by the French government's refusal to approve.

Deane seems never to have given the De Broglie matter more than a passing thought. Deane's respect and admiration for General Washington was well known. In 1775 Deane had advocated the appointment of George Washington for the post of Commander-in-Chief of the American army. To his wife, Deane often expressed his admiration of Washington and felt honored when the General accepted his invitation to spend the night in Deane's home in Wethersfield as he traveled to Cambridge to take command of the Continental Army. Unfortunately for Deane, his countrymen considered the mere recommendation of Washington's replacement by a Frenchman as an affront that could never be forgotten or forgiven.

The correspondence of men in Congress and the observations of foreign visitors indicate that the foreign officers in America caused the single greatest resentment against Deane and were probably the greatest factor leading to his recall by Congress.[48] Deane used poor judgment in selecting the number of officers and setting out the terms of their contracts. It is possible that he was playing for higher stakes than Congress appreciated. He was concerned with public support in France; the French officers were influential in society. Deane, and later Franklin, grasped that in France where public meetings were prohibited, public opinion formed and expressed itself in less obvious ways, of which private volunteering was one. John Adams and Arthur Lee never did understand this, and as a result failed to interpret many of Deane's motives and moves.

Apart from his mistakes in choosing French officers, there were concerted efforts by British officials to discredit Deane. Shortly after he arrived in France, a rope factory and the docks of Portsmouth burned. A John Atkins, alias John the Painter, was arrested and accused of the crime. Admitting his guilt in open court, he stated he had been hired by Silas Deane, rebel agent in Paris. There was some truth in Atkins's testimony.[49] Atkins was correct when he said he had visited Deane in Paris. But that Deane had hired him is doubtful; a British agent in Paris well acquainted with Deane questioned the idea.[50] Still, the trial received great publicity in London, perhaps with some careful sponsorship.

Another effort to discredit the American agent with the French government came in the closing days of 1777. By that time negotiations between the Revolutionary Commissioners and the French government were at a delicate stage. M. Favier, well-known to the Paris police as a person of unsavory reputation, was requested to review and report on the activities of his former associate, the British agent, Paul Wentworth. The latter was then suspected of being an agent in Paris, and Vergennes was curious about his activities. Wentworth told Favier that he and Deane were old friends and often "supped together with a woman whom he believed to be his [Deane's] mistress." He stated that Deane had transferred money to Wentworth's relatives in America. He casually mentioned he had suggested financial and commercial speculations to Deane and that Deane "refused it . . . not out of scruple, but because he was engaged with Messrs. Grand, Beaumarchais and Panchaud who transacted business in funds; and who had admitted him into their speculations and profits."[51] Wentworth's motives were apparent. Favier, however, did not consider this particular story especially reliable. To Vergennes he wrote: "If this tale about Mr. Deane is true, you are certainly aware of it" already.[52]

It is interesting to speculate that such stories might have been originated by British agents with the intention of circulating them until they reached the ears of Congress through Arthur Lee or some other American, for in this way they could dispose of the man in Paris whom they considered dangerous. Deane obviously worried the British greatly, more so than his other compatriots in Paris, including Benjamin Franklin. In a report marked "confidential," Stormont expressed his belief that "Whatever his [Franklin's] talents . . . I am persuaded that he is a less dangerous instrument than Deane."[53] There is no proof that the British government had a direct hand in Deane's recall by Congress. Even so, that British agents were in and around Congress was a matter beyond question, and if they wanted to dispose of him they must—it may be assumed—have tried to attack his reputation. In discussing Deane's recall, Chaumont later observed to Vergennes: "If we compare dates, we find the recall of Mr. Deane coincides with the period when Lord North was able to intrigue in Congress, guided by what he had read in the despatches he had caused to be stolen. Mr. Deane's head was a good one for him to strike."[54]

CHAPTER 3

AS MEMBER

OF THE PARIS COMMISSION

SILAS Deane's status changed in December 1776 when he became a member of a three-man commission vested with full diplomatic power. The commission reflected the decision of Congress to seek military aid from France in the war against Great Britain. Congress was willing to enter into a formal alliance. Here was a new course in the conduct of the war, and Deane was to play an important if not conspicuous role in this new policy.

The congressional decision to request foreign intervention in a heretofore purely family quarrel was not taken without searching debate. While Deane was arranging for supplies in France during the latter half of 1776, Congress argued the virtues of a purely commercial alliance against those of a political-military alliance. The deteriorating military situation was decisive in crystallizing congressional opinion. Deane's instructions of March 3, 1776, from the Committee of Secret Correspondence ordered him to test French reaction to an alliance and to the proposed Declaration of Independence. In reports to the Committee, Deane repeatedly requested permission to press the French ministers for an alliance, but both the Committee of Secret Correspondence and Congress remained silent on this subject.[1]

Congressional fears and indecision during this critical period were revealed in the thoughts and words of Benjamin Franklin, Thomas Paine, and

John Adams. All careful men, evaluating the needs of the moment, they considered the effect of each day's action on future events. As late as July 1775 Franklin wrote to a friend in England: "We have not applied to any foreign power for assistance nor offered our commerce for this friendship."[2] Franklin knew that war and independence meant that America must leave the British mercantile system. He was keenly aware that to carry on war the colonies had to trade; on February 26, 1776, he introduced a resolution providing for the opening of American ports to "ships of all countries."[3] Fearful of a permanent rupture and still unwilling to face such drastic action against Great Britain, Congress resisted the resolution until April 6.

In *Common Sense* Thomas Paine likewise had presented a political and commercial policy to the colonists. Maintaining that it was in the interest of all the European countries to have America a free port, Paine wrote that commerce would protect the United Colonies and would secure Europe's friendship with America. However, "As Europe is our market for trade, we ought to form no partial connection with any part of it. It is the true interest of America to steer clear of European countentions, which she never can do, while, by her dependence on Britain, she is made the makeweight in the scale of British politics."[4]

John Adams advocated a simple commercial treaty; when the time came to formulate a proposed treaty with France he defended his exclusively commercial position both in committee and in open debate in Congress.[5]

Richard Henry Lee's triple motion in Congress on June 7, 1776, for independence, confederation, and "the most effectual measures for forming foreign Alliances" forced a decision.[6] A committee was appointed to draft terms for an eventual commercial treaty and submit it to Congress for approval. John Adams once again warned that such an alliance might involve the nation in Europe's wars. He stressed that such a treaty would repeal the Navigation Acts and bring France into American commerce. If France should become involved in the war by supplying the colonies with goods and recognizing their independence, he thought, she would find ample compensation in American trade.[7] During the debates, Adams opposed his "own intimate friends, Samuel Adams and Richard Henry Lee." The latter thought that American commerce was insufficient reward for France to join the colonies and moved for cessions and concessions that implied "warranties and a political alliance" which Adams had sought to avoid.[8] The instructions Franklin carried to Paris authorized only a commercial alliance.

If John Adams and his policy won the first round, Samuel Adams and Richard Henry Lee won the second round in October 1776, when they convinced Congress to empower the commissioners in Paris to seek recognition from other European courts. An additional victory for them came in December when Congress appointed commissioners to the courts of Spain, Austria, Prussia, and Tuscany.

The original members appointed to the commission to France were Benjamin Franklin, Thomas Jefferson, and Silas Deane. Jefferson refused to serve; and Arthur Lee, who was stationed in London, was appointed in his place.

Silas Deane, in Paris as agent of the Committee of Secret Correspondence, had status both at home and in France. He had done the preliminary work for the other two members. Both Franklin and Lee received instructions to proceed immediately to Paris and assume responsibilities, both present and future, starting from Deane's initial activities for the conduct of American affairs.

Benjamin Franklin was seventy years old when selected for the new assignment, and accepted the mission without regard to health, discomfort, or financial loss. During the succeeding nine years he was in France he received only his salary, and on it he lived. He was responsible for handling thousands of dollars, yet when his accounts were audited not one instance of mismanagement appeared against him. Franklin was thoroughly familiar with the politics of two continents. As colonial postmaster he had traveled into every inhabited area of the American colonies. For forty years he had been active in Pennsylvania politics. He had favored several plans of colonial alliance or union. He had been agent in England for Pennsylvania, Massachusetts, New Jersey, and Georgia. No American was more familiar with British politics. He had first encountered France as an antagonist when the colonists supported Great Britain during the colonial wars of 1740–48 and 1754–63. In 1767 he had visited Paris and made many friends. When he returned in 1776, he found himself an honored and beloved guest. "Social France received him as an idol; philosophical France received him as a co-worker in a great work; military France greeted him as an ally against an old foe; commercial France at once set him down as a means of netting considerable sums and all alike welcomed him warmly."[9] His reception by the French ministers, while not official, was extremely cordial. During 1777, however, Franklin's diplomacy was primarily with the French people.

The third member of the Paris Commission, Arthur Lee, a native of Virginia, received his early formal education at Eton College, England. He secured a medical degree at Edinburgh. After travel on the continent he returned to Virginia to practice, but dissatisfied he returned to England and studied law from 1766 until 1770.

As a patriot, Arthur Lee ranked second to none. His bitter enemies, of whom there were many, acknowledged his loyalty. But neither by training nor by temperament was Arthur Lee suited for public life. Lee admitted that "Unhappily my fate has thrown me into public life, and the impatience of my nature makes me embark in it with an impetuosity and imprudence which increase the evils to which it is necessarily subject."[10] John Adams, inclined to suspicion, said that Arthur Lee "had confidence in nobody, believed all men selfish, and no man honest or sincere."[11] Beaumarchais described him as an "insidious politician."[12] Benjamin Franklin had earlier contact with Arthur Lee in London and thought him half-crazy, an evaluation Silas Deane was to think generous.[13]

Arthur Lee, like his brother, William Lee, had learned politics from John Wilkes, whose vituperative language appears in their correspondence. Suspicion was inherent in Arthur Lee's character. If he met a person he could not dominate or whose thinking he could not bend, he convinced himself that some plot was afoot. Arthur Lee conceived the notion that all Deane's friends must be his enemies. Plots, intrigues, and combinations marred his character and injured his reputation. He believed that adversaries wrote paragraphs to his discredit, inserted them in European gazettes, and saw that they were repeated in the American papers. He thought his enemies were busy writing letters to poison not only the public mind but the minds of individuals whose opinions were important to his success.

Alone, Arthur Lee might have been ineffective, but as a member of a powerful family with political and social connections he was a factor not safely ignored. John Jay traced the failure of the colonies' naval affairs to a Lee "family compact." Brothers of the family held two seats in Congress, four foreign missions, the American commercial agency in France, and a London aldermanship. Moreover, many New England delegates sympathized with the views of Richard and Arthur Lee. James Lovell, self-styled "Mr. Secretary" of the Foreign Affairs Committee, was active in presenting the family view. Samuel Adams consistently supported the Lees.

Such a combination was formidable. It is doubtful that any of the Lee brothers was guilty of disloyalty to the Revolution, but such was their loyalty to each other that it ill-served any man to oppose them. Beaumarchais, Deane, and even Benjamin Franklin gained the hatred of Arthur Lee and thereby the enmity of the Lee brothers. Beaumarchais died a pauper, and Deane in disgrace; Franklin was subjected to a barrage of bitter personal and political charges by Arthur Lee and company that continued even after his death.[14]

Franklin obviously was the most important member of the commission. When he landed in France, he missed Vergennes's messenger warning him not to come to Paris. After his arrival in the capital, he stayed for some weeks at the Hôtel d'Hambourg in the Rue de Université, but later moved to an "elegant hotel" in Passy just outside Paris, belonging to Monsieur de Chaumont. As the house was offered rent free, it is not difficult to detect the fine hand of Vergennes, who realized that Franklin would dominate the thinking of his companions and probably wished to keep him out of the capital. Franklin's headquarters in Passy soon became the nerve center of all American diplomatic activity in France. The house served as chancery, lodging, and social center for Franklin and Deane. Arthur Lee maintained a separate establishment. By common consent, Franklin became the unofficial but recognized "head of mission." The British ambassador, Lord Stormont, referred to him as "chief of the rebels." And Arthur Lee's opinion to the contrary, Franklin was an able diplomat. Even a casual examination of his reports to Congress shows his awareness of issues.

The organization of the commission in Paris was simple and informal. The commissioners were handicapped in routine affairs because Congress had failed to provide for administrative assistants. Franklin's only personal assistant was his sixteen-year-old grandson, William Temple Franklin. Although a good copyist, he could not be entrusted with drafting the many papers Franklin had to write. Dr. Edward Bancroft, the double spy, and William Carmichael, the ambitious young man from Maryland, did some of the clerical work, but had no legal status and were not part of the official family.

[32]

The commission had difficulties other than clerical. Although the mission ended in ultimate success, it was accompanied by strain and uncertainty, punctuated by personal rivalry and jealousy. A portion of the difficulty was the problem of negotiation. The prime difficulty resulted from the failure of Congress to delineate the respective responsibilities of the individual commissioners. Their instructions made them jointly responsible, but any two could make an official agreement. All American affairs outside the colonies, unless otherwise delegated by Congress, were under their jurisdiction. None of the commissioners was a trained professional diplomat. With limited diplomatic experience, without precedents and without adequate staff, they had a difficult assignment.

The French government refused officially to recognize the American commission, but within a few days Vergennes received Franklin and his colleagues in a private but not secret audience. They presented their letter of credence, the draft of a proposed treaty of commerce, and a request for eight warships to convoy merchant ships to America. Vergennes denied the request for ships. Such an act would mean that France openly espoused the cause of the Americans, and would have brought immediate war with Great Britain.[15] He said the time was inopportune for war. His reception of the proposed treaty of commerce was equally disappointing, for the minister agreed only to take the idea under advisement. France was not yet ready to recognize the United Colonies. American commerce was the only advantage or inducement the commissioners had to offer; as Great Britain dominated the ocean between America and France, this was a doubtful gain. Nor was the military situation encouraging. The British army had taken New York City and threatened Philadelphia. The rumor in French official circles was that Burgoyne was starting south from Canada.

After their reception by Vergennes, and having accepted the extended protection of the French court, the commissioners retired to plan their next move.

Meanwhile, Lee decided to visit the courts of Madrid, Vienna, and Berlin. Franklin did not approve, but consented. Lee left Paris in February 1777 and spent the spring and summer months in an unsuccessful quest for aid and recognition.

Gradually, the commission in Paris settled into a routine. Franklin conducted diplomacy primarily through social intercourse. A barrage of letters went from Passy to persons of all classes and stations in French society. The old philosopher dined out, entertained, and attended the Academy of Science. Parisians were always conscious that the American was in their midst. Routine liaison work was left to Deane. Franklin refused to assume responsibility for commitments resulting from Deane's arrangements or contracts; these Deane concluded on his own. Beaumarchais wrote concerning the new arrangements. On January 6, 1777, Deane replied that the joint commission in no way interfered with his former instructions to purchase and ship supplies to America and "my Colleagues will not intermeddle in the Engagements taken by me previous to their Arrival. The whole, therefore, of this affair remains in the state it was at first, and it lyes soley on us to take the best measure in our power to get the Shipps to Sea with the Stores as soon as possible.[16] Deane, in fact, served as Franklin's detail and "leg man." The commissioners had to solicit the court of France for an immediate supply of war materials. "This application has now become the more necessary, as the private purchase made by Mr. Deane of those articles is rendered ineffectual by an order forbidding their exportation."[17]

New contracts or arrangements from December 1776 on were under Franklin's direction. Deane immediately accepted Franklin as "Chief of Mission," and the two worked in harmony and understanding. By mutual consent, Deane also served as the contact man between Franklin and Vergennes. The old philosopher was too much in the public eye for Vergennes's idea of secret diplomacy, and the French Foreign Minister distrusted Arthur Lee even before the commission was formed.

CHAPTER 4

DEANE

AND AMERICAN COMMERCE

THE failure of Congress to define each commissioner's duties and responsibilities eventually led to an explosive situation. While Arthur Lee traveled
and Franklin pursued his social diplomacy, Deane assumed responsibility
for the commission's commercial activities. Roughly, the commercial department included privateering and prizes, naval affairs, and shared pro-
curement and shipping of supplies with a civil agency at Nantes possessing
ill-defined powers from Congress. That such an arrangement caused trouble
is not surprising, but that it produced any good results whatsoever is
nothing less than remarkable.

As agent of the Secret Committee of Correspondence, Deane had taken
an interest in privateering. Upon arriving in France, he realized the harm
privateers could do English commerce and what a source of revenue their
capture could become for the treasury of the United Colonies. In reports
to the Committee, he requested Congress to send blank commissions so that
he might authorize American privateers to prey on British ships.[1] Franklin
brought orders to buy eight ships of line. Captain Wickes, commander of
the *Reprisal* on which Franklin had sailed to France, had captured two
prizes on the trip and escorted them to port. Franklin designated Wickes
to investigate ships and make recommendations for purchases. Wickes did

a thorough job. However, even when the commissioners had money to buy ships, they discovered that purchase was only the beginning of difficulties. The selection of officers, sailors, merchants to fit out the ships, and cruises to be made when the ships were ready, presented a complicated set of problems. None of the commissioners had experience in maritime affairs; yet each had to act almost as a department of the navy. As a merchant and former member of the congressional naval committee, Deane was the best equipped to take charge of this operation.

Deane's commercial duties produced Anglo-French difficulties. The statute of neutral nations under international custom, later called public international law, did not cause the Americans as much trouble as it did the French government. Among the more complicated questions, the following disturbed the British and embarrassed the French: (1) were American warships and privateers to be allowed in French ports? (2) could privateers sail from neutral ports, take prizes, and return? (3) was it legal for English sailors captured at sea to be confined in French ports and later exchanged for American prisoners in England? France and Great Britain had treaty arrangements on these points, a fact recognized by the French ministers, and Lord Stormont's evidence was so clear that Vergennes had to delay rather than evade these issues of neutrality.

The French government publicly proclaimed its neutrality in 1777. The Treaty of Utrecht in 1714 between Great Britain and France spelled out the duties of a neutral.

In spite of Stormont's ability to cite constant violation of this treaty, the French ministers were slow to act. Handling Stormont's complaints was reduced to a formula. Vergennes would plead ignorance of facts, but promise an immediate investigation. In due time he would request information from the Minister of Marine, who would reply that he had no information but would inquire of officials at the port in question. By the time Vergennes would be in position to give Stormont an answer, the ship would have finished refitting and left port. If the privateers were so slow or unlucky as to be in port, the French would order it to leave in twenty-four hours—it must transfer to another port. The French minister winked at violations. Vergennes was willing to match wits with Stormont, though not to the extent of risking war with Great Britain. He would write a severe reprimand to the American commissioners for some act, but drastic action never followed.[2] In principle, the Americans agreed with Vergennes, but the commissioners did not promise nor intend to cease their activities. They were, it has been observed, "a thick-skinned gentry, who well understood that hard words break no bones and with whom measures to be effective had to be drastic."[3]

In time, France did take semidrastic steps to curb her would-be ally, but not until the British put French ports under an unofficial blockade. Vergennes explained to Chaumont, in whose house Deane and Franklin lived, that they would not be pleased with the course taken in regard to their privateers but it was indispensable at that moment; moreover, there was no question of vexing anyone, only of assuring the British that privateers would cease to infest French seas.

In March 1777, before the French court was forced to take action, Deane and a fellow American, William Hodge, conceived the idea of fitting out an American privateer in Dunkirk which would make a prize of the Harwick packet. Arthur Lee was in Spain, and it is doubtful if Franklin had much to do with the affair. Deane is the only commissioner listed in the papers, and evidently attended to all details. The scheme was not only bold but successful. Deane and Hodge purchased a lugger at Dover, through a Captain Cruise. The ship was taken to Dunkirk and under Hodge's direction fitted out for the expedition which was to be under the command of Gustavus Conyngham, who held a Continental commission as Captain. With ease, Captain Conyngham captured both the Harwick mail packet and a brig. He brazenly returned with his prizes to Dunkirk, his point of departure. The affair caused excitement in official circles in both England and France. Conyngham was immediately arrested, and the prizes confiscated. Much to the satisfaction of the English court, France promised that Conyngham should be given up, the prizes restored, and nothing of this nature again allowed.

That the Americans did not take these occasional French moves against privateering seriously became evident. When the packet boat and brig were returned to the British, Deane remarked it "gave them a temporary triumph."[4] Deane and Hodge determined to seize the Harwick packet again. They fitted out another cutter with fourteen six-pounders and twenty-two swivels. Upon representation that he was to sail directly to America, Conyngham and his crew were released from prison. Hodge gave bond. To avoid mishap, the French government offered to buy the vessel, but the offer was refused and the vessel sailed on "a trading voyage." No sooner was the cutter out of port than Conyngham proceeded to make a prize of everything he met, even threatening to burn the English city of Linn.[5] Because he did not return to a French port, nothing was said directly to the commissioners. His surety, Hodge, was arrested and sent to the Bastille, but discharged when Deane, acting for the commissioners, stated he was a man of character and could not "conceive him capable of any willful offense against the Laws of this nation."[6]

Similar incidents, many times multiplied, demonstrated the range of American privateering, in which French ministers connived. Rarely were there less than a dozen ship captains receiving hospitality at the unofficial headquarters of Passy. Arthur Lee, upon returning from Spain, was distressed by what he considered Franklin and Deane's display of nonchalance in the face of French hospitality. This he believed a threat to eventual alliance.[7] In later months both Arthur and William Lee brought this episode forward in their attempt to discredit Deane and Franklin.[8]

Meanwhile, there had arisen the case of Thomas Morris, Robert Morris's half-brother, who became the commercial agent in Nantes. He also served as agent for Willing and Morris, a commercial firm of Philadelphia. In the latter capacity, he was independent of the commissioners in Paris. But Deane, supported by Franklin, drew a distinction between commercial and naval jurisdiction. Deane and Franklin, but not Arthur Lee, included privateering and the sale of prizes under the jurisdiction of the commissioners in Paris.[9]

Thomas Morris proved a drunkard and incompetent. Deane, and later the commissioners collectively, informed Robert Morris and the Secret Committee of Correspondence of Thomas Morris's "irregularities" and recommended that he be replaced. A month later, Arthur Lee, while in Spain, wrote his brother, Richard Henry, in Congress that "the superintendent general of the commerce is immersed, and has been ever since his coming over, in the lowest debauchery and scottishness. Irrecoverably and notoriously so. Think then, how much your commercial interests must suffer in the hands of two such men. . . . The Alderman in London [William Lee, their brother] would be the best controller general of your commerce that could possibly be found."[10]

With or without Arthur Lee's advice, the Secret Committee of Correspondence informed Deane that William Lee of London had been appointed joint-commercial agent at Nantes with Thomas Morris. William Lee was a successful merchant in London, staunch supporter of John Wilkes of that city, and had been elected alderman with Wilkes' support and endorsement. For unknown reasons, William Lee did not surrender his British aldermanship until forced to do so. If William Lee failed to render service to the Revolution, it was not because he lacked office and status. He was simultaneously alderman of the City of London, commercial agent at Nantes, and commissioner to the Vienna and Berlin courts. As ordered, Deane wrote in the name of the commission informing William Lee of his new appointment in Nantes.

Because of personal affairs, Alderman Lee did not arrive in Paris until June 1777. No instructions had come from Philadelphia to Paris or to William Lee; therefore, William Lee decided to be inactive pending his commission. Not permitted to visit either Vienna or Berlin, he spent most of his time in Paris complaining that the other commissioners did not consult him, and writing his brother in Congress opinions on the administration of sundry congressional affairs which, he felt, would be better under his jurisdiction. Then he clashed with Deane and Franklin over the commercial agency at Nantes. His theme was that Deane and Franklin were exceeding their authority and were more interested in private than public business.

William Lee retained an active interest in stockjobbing while drawing money from the American treasury. He remained in Paris from June to August, waiting for a commercial commission that never came. Then, at the request of Deane and Franklin, he went to Nantes to see if he could bring order into the affairs of that center of American commerce.

The affairs at Nantes had become so critical that action was necessary. Outfitting privateers and selling prizes required an intelligent and able man who could anticipate and evade the orders of port officials. Robert Morris sent John Ross from Philadelphia to investigate the affairs of Willing and Morris and Company and if necessary to take charge. In May 1777 Deane, with Franklin's permission, asked Jonathan Williams to go to Nantes and take charge of the privateering business, supplanting and superseding Thomas Morris. He was so satisfactory that Deane retained him, although he knew William Lee expected to serve as co-agent of this public commercial business at Nantes. He confirmed his decision to Williams: "Mr. Lee's arrival would make no odds in this business, as it is distinct from anything contained in either of their appointments, and your appointment from us is the only one at present that can be of any force . . ."[11]

Morris resented and protested his suspension, arguing that his commission from the Committee of Secret Correspondence placed the sale of prizes under his jurisdiction. Deane, although worried, did not alter his decision, and as long as he was in France the naval affairs of the port remained with Jonathan Williams.

A new element came in July 1777 when John Ross wrote Deane from Nantes:

> Permit me now to inform you, Mr. Morris is possessed of the Instructions of Mr. Lee, from Committee of Congress, on his being appointed Commercial Agent here. . . . These instructions are contained in a letter addressed to Mr. Lee and Mr. Morris as Joint Agents, which is similar and of equal force with the separate powers on which Mr. Morris acted hitherto. I therefore take the liberty to recommend Mr. Lee's repairing hither immediately, to assume the Management, being certain Mr. Morris will possess him of this letter, so soon as they meet, tho' kept so long back, probably from inattention.[12]

Deane then knew, but did not inform William Lee, that Morris had Lee's instructions from the Committee. At this time and after leaving Paris for Nantes, William Lee was on the best of terms with Deane. He wrote Deane on August 12: "I will write you on business as soon as those that have hitherto been concerned here will permit me to enter on any, which has not been the case as yet, nor indeed have I been able to procure a sight of any letter, instructions or papers whatsoever relative to the business."[13] As long as Alderman Lee was in Nantes, he found that neither his presence nor advice was desired or followed. He returned to Paris. When he learned of Thomas Morris's letter, he wrote his brother, Richard Henry Lee, that Silas Deane had suspended him too, "though he knows perfectly well that the sale of prizes was expressly committed to Mr. Morris and myself by the Secret Committee."[14] To his brother, Francis Lightfoot Lee, he complained: "In the First Line I cou'd & shou'd have been of great [use] unto the Public, as well as myself; especially if the Secret Committee wou'd support their own Authority & show an insolent meddler here [Deane] that they wd properly notice his presumption in taking on himself in many instances to contravene their appointments and orders."[15]

The battle of the Nantes commercial agency continued. To reassure Williams of the legality of his position, Franklin wrote: "You need have no concern as your orders being only from Mr. Deane . . . but as he generally consulted with me and had my approbation in the orders he gave, and I know they were for the best aimed at the public good, I hereby certify you that I approve and join in these you have received from him, and desire you to proceed in the execution of the same."[16]

Deane wrote Robert Morris in September 1777, describing Williams as "generous and disinterested."[17] To maintain surface harmony, Deane proposed, and Franklin agreed, that all commercial transactions and naval business should return to Thomas Morris and William Lee, but afterward Arthur Lee refused to sign the letter or permit it to be sent. His excuse was that as William Lee meantime had been appointed commissioner to the courts of Berlin and Vienna he would be leaving for this post.

The "battle of the agents" seemed over when word came that Thomas Morris was dead. Upon the advice of the three commissioners, William Lee went to Nantes to prevent the French from seizing Morris's papers. To Francis Lightfoot Lee, William wrote that he was going to Nantes to take charge of the papers and "to form some plan for conducting the public commercial business as I am immediately going on my Embassy in Germany."[18]

Instead of solving the problem of the commercial agency, Morris's death aggravated the situation. John Ross informed Deane that William Lee spent four days secretly going through Morris's public and private papers. Later, William Lee requested three American merchants in Nantes to certify that he had selected only the public papers. The merchants refused, and as Ross described the situation to Deane, their champion was "so chagrined and mortified on receiving their answer, that his passion and dignity forced him to a declaration, that the papers (as they lay in the trunk) should be carried to Paris, and put in the hands of the commissioners." In the same letter Ross wrote that "a Letter of yours selected with many others is said here to have made discoverys of great imposition on the public." He assured Deane of permission to use his name to refute any "strained constructions and malicious insinuations" which might be made against Deane.[19]

The affairs of the Nantes commercial agency passed under the control of William Lee. Naval affairs remained under Jonathan Williams's direction until Deane sailed for America. Planning to leave for Germany, William Lee offered partnership in the agency to Williams, but upon Franklin's advice Williams declined. Lee appointed as subagent William Schweighauser, a German merchant residing in Nantes. His nephew, Thomas Lee, son of Richard Henry Lee, became clerk. Informed of this arrangement by William Lee, Deane wrote: "I can have no objection to the Persons you propose appointing to act under you in the Commercial Agency, nor can I take any active part in that affair." In the same letter Deane requested that as he would return to America before Lee's return to France, Lee should inform him before either left France of any imputations of this nature Lee had authorized.[20] To John Ross he wrote:

> I should be very happy could I bring my Enemies here into open day, and to lay their accusations and complaints against me formally, in which case I should know what I had to answer to: but this I despair of, for he only who made them can alter their dispositions; it is very hard to be obliged to combat such bush fighting Poltroons, against whom one can never be too much on one's Defence, and never sure for a moment, but I trust soon to Lug them all out in to open day.[21]

When the commission was formally organized in December 1776, it was natural that Deane control the commercial and financial departments because of his experience and contacts. He was popular with French ministers and had channels of communication. He enjoyed wide acquaintances in French mercantile circles. Still, he had great trouble settling affairs with Beaumarchais. While Deane was having difficulties with the commercial agency, his friend Beaumarchais was having trouble because of Congress's failure to send remittances. A French restraining order made it difficult for Beaumarchais to forward supplies. Also, because of the French government's refusal to permit ships to sail, Beaumarchais arrived at the point of bankruptcy. After many passionate but unsuccessful appeals to Vergennes for relief, he sent his nephew, Theveneau de Francey, to America in September, 1777, to investigate the congressional failure. From there De Francey warned Beaumarchais he would never be paid and to "trim his financial sails." "There is no doubt that what you have done has been presented here in a false light. I expect to have many prejudices to destroy and many heads to set right, for the sending of several vessels without invoices (a thing which, to say the truth is unprecedented), and the errors found in the bill of lading of the *Amphitrite,* especially, have caused it to be suspected that the shipments were not by a merchant."[22] In spite of these warnings, Beaumarchais negotiated a second contract with Congress. Congress still did not pay for the supplies received under the old contract with Deane, apparently preferring to accept Arthur Lee's assurances that Beaumarchais was the agent of the king of France and expected no remittance for the supplies.

Deane continued to support Beaumarchais. His report of September 3, 1777, praised Beaumarchais for sending supplies and urged payment for goods received. "Whatever this ship *Heureuse* may be loaded with, I pray the cargo may come to Messrs. Rodrigue Hortalez & Co., as they have advanced for the arms and other articles of this cargo over and above their other large advances."[23]

When the *Amphitrite* arrived in France loaded with a cargo of rice, indigo, and tobacco, Beaumarchais demanded that the cargo be turned over. Arthur Lee declared that he had never heard of any agreement made with him, and Franklin expressed surprise that money was demanded of them for goods they never ordered and that "Mr. Deane seemed unacquainted with any agreement with him." Later the commissioners informed Congress that Beaumarchais had satisfied them that he had a claim upon the cargo of the *Amphitrite* according to an agreement between him and Deane. The commissioners recommended that Beaumarchais's accounts be settled in France because of the "mixture of public and private business."[24] Reporting the affair to Vergennes, Beaumarchais spoke of that "honest deputy, Mr. Deane" and later repeated that "one of my greatest encouragements is the gratitude of that honest man, speaking for his nation."[25]

The Beaumarchais affair was embarrassing. Both Arthur and William Lee insinuated that Deane engaged extensively in private business while serving as an agent of the Secret Committee of Correspondence and commissioner of Congress in France, but they did not cite specific cases. Deane was informing friends, but not complaining, of the burden of his office. In

October 1777 he wrote the congressional delegate from Virginia, Benjamin Harrison, that he was so engaged in "procuring Cloathing [sic] and other Supplies for the public, the laborious part which was lain on me," that he did not have the energy to take advantage of his knowledge of the European business world to engage in ventures of a private nature.[26] In January 1778 Deane confided to Robert Morris, his accused partner in speculation, that he found it impossible to attend any private venture because of the press of duties. For the first time he expressed a desire to "quit Politics forever" and attend solely to his private affairs, which had been neglected for several years.[27] On the eve of departure for America in March 1778 he wrote John Ross that two of the three commercial adventures in which he, Robert Morris, Beaumarchais, Delap, and Chaumont had participated were complete losses. The third was profitable.[28] That he included these transactions later in oral and written reports to Congress indicated that he did not consider them of importance.

Deane's enemies charged that he shipped inferior goods to America and in general was casual with the public business. But Deane was operating without staff, from widely separated ports, and with a variety of cargoes. Communication and transport were poor, complaints from America scarce. His accusers failed to produce proof for the charges. Even William Lee did not object at that time to Deane's business practices; he also failed to avail himself of Deane's invitation "to inform me previous to either of our leaving France of any imputations of this nature which you have authorized against me."[29]

That Deane did the best he could is apparent; through his correspondence run orders and warnings to agents to use every care and precaution to protect the public interest. As early as January 1777 he informed Beaumarchais of rumors that "arms and other articles" for shipment from Le Havre and Nantes were inferior and improperly crated. He feared that "certain busy persons" were circulating these rumors. He proposed that William Carmichael go to Le Havre and Jonathan Williams to Nantes to "examine personally into the state of the arms and stores" and if everything was satisfactory to remain until the ships had sailed. Beaumarchais's reply mentioned these "inspections of arms and merchandise . . . which have served to refute all base suspicions which have feigned as to the excellence of the articles furnished." Beaumarchais complained that he did not think

Commissioner Deane need be so exacting when he had not fulfilled commitments to him.[30]

His correspondence with other contractors also helps refute the talk that Deane had permitted inferior goods to go to America. He expected to receive quality merchandise and at a fair price. Williams, Deane's agent at Nantes, was to check the quality of uniforms to be delivered for shipment. "I have only to caution you how to receive them, if they will not fully answer the comparison with those sent by Messrs. Holker and Co.," he should reject them. Shortly before he returned to America he informed the firm of Geradot and Halber that he could not accept the uniforms on any account.[31]

Nor is there any evidence of military dissatisfaction with the materials Deane sent. One of the first persons to express appreciation upon Deane's return to the United States in July 1778 was General Washington, who should have been aware of any inferiorities in supplies.[32]

In the autumn of 1777 when Arthur Lee returned to Paris from the courts of Madrid, Vienna, and Berlin, his requests for aid and recognition rebuffed, differences among the commissioners appeared. According to instructions, the commissioners were collectively responsible for decisions of the commission, but each was accountable to Congress for the financial transactions to which he was party. Such a division of power permitted Deane and Franklin to prevent legal settlement of accounts or explanation for individual accounts. In his report to Congress, Deane maintained that Lee knew of all contracts and expenditures. Lee maintained he did not. To his brother, Richard Henry, Lee complained that "Mr. Deane, Dr. Bancroft, and William Carmichael . . . have been practicing against me, and what I do not know is how far it may extend."[33] Division of responsibility may justify Arthur Lee's warnings that something should be done to protect the public interest, but does not explain his desire to acquire control of the commission.

Returning to Paris, Lee charged failure to press the French for an alliance, endangering and violating French neutrality and hospitality, indiscriminate privateering, open and illegal sale of prizes in French ports, and mishandling of affairs.[34] William Lee, alderman of London, commercial agent at Nantes, and commissioner at the Courts of Vienna and Berlin, supported his brother in these accusations. Arthur Lee maintained that

[45]

during his journeys the commissioners had failed to inform him of affairs. He was critical of the business of the privateers and charged that sums had been spent without his knowledge and consent. William Lee's difficulties with the commercial agency at Nantes did nothing to calm tempers. Deane's midnight visits to Versailles for conferences with Gérard and Vergennes added to Arthur Lee's suspicion that matters were concealed from him, that state secrets were used for private commercial advantages. Such a condition was too much for a man who desired to accomplish great things for his country. Arthur Lee convinced himself he was the victim of a cabal by Deane, abetted by Franklin, to deprive him of honor and credit. To his congressional friend, Theodoric Bland, he admitted he resented the attempt to deny him "that praise that constant toil and assiduity in the public service had deserved." He accused, without naming, one of his colleagues of making sixty thousand pounds by using public money and state secrets in private trading.[35]

Lee was no man to suffer defeat gracefully. When he discovered that neither Franklin nor Deane would accept his leadership or criticism, he conceived a plan to control the Paris mission. What he could not win in Paris by merit he could achieve in Philadelphia by maneuver. In early fall of 1777 he wrote Samuel Adams reviewing the political capitals he had visited. He believed France "the great wheel" that controlled all Europe, and if there were ever question in Congress as to his future assignment he would be "much obliged" to Adams for remembering "I prefer being at the Court of France."[36] On October 4 he wrote Richard Henry Lee, chairman of the Secret Committee of Correspondence, suggesting that Congress assign Franklin to Vienna and Deane to The Hague. Lee justified his plan on the need of adapting "Characters and Places," and as France was the center of political activity he felt he should remain in Paris.[37] This plan of adapting "Characters and Places" was, as he admitted, designed to give control of the most important diplomatic post in Europe to himself. When Congress failed to see merit in his plan, Lee returned to the charge of dissension, neglect, dissipation, and private schemes in an attempt to discredit his colleagues. In January 1778 he once more appealed to Richard Henry Lee, pointing out that he was responsible for things he could not prevent. "There is but one way of redressing this and remedying the public evil; that is the plan I before sent you."[38]

Arthur Lee never doubted his ability to operate the "great wheel" in Paris. Yet he was cautious about citing cases of graft, corruption, and speculation. His "whispers" in Samuel Adams' ear of stockjobbing by his colleagues did not constitute proof.[39]

Knowledge of Lee's suspicion of his colleagues was not limited to friends and brothers in America. In a letter intercepted by the General Post Office in London, William Carmichael, no friend of either the Lees or Deane, wrote that "The misfortune of these people is to believe that everybody is plotting against them, they therefore plot against everybody. They think me leagues with Mr. Deane and Dr. F[ranklin] at the very time I really feel hurt at their public conduct and the private behavior of one to myself."[40]

It would have been unusual if Deane had not lost his temper or resented what he considered unfair and unjust criticism. The entire time Deane lived in France was a period of high tension. Deane was sensitive to his colleague's charges and insinuations of mismanagement and private speculation. He wrote a straightforward letter to Arthur Lee on December 13, 1777, asking for a meeting. In the public interest he invited his colleague to tell him frankly the "grounds for all his uneasiness" and promised he would give any information he desired." This way, Deane concluded, "[is] certainly a more honorable and just way, between equals at least, than Private insinuations and threatening Billets or Complaining ones."[41] Arthur Lee did not answer. Negotiations with the French court soon became the dominant concern of the commissioners and personal animosities were temporarily forgotten.

The signing of the Treaty of Amity and Commerce and the Treaty of Alliance in March 1778 ended the French policy of "watchful waiting." The policy of secret aid had ended with formal recognition of the colonies.

CHAPTER 5

DEANE

AND AMERICAN DIPLOMACY

LONG before Silas Deane arrived in France in July 1776 the French ministers had watched the war in America with interest. Louis XVI and his cabinet carefully considered means of sustaining the conflict without becoming involved until an American victory was assured. As the tide of battle favored the British early in 1776, the French government adopted a policy of waiting, while encouraging the rebels with secret aid. General Burgoyne's surrender at Saratoga on October 17, 1777, convinced the French ministers that the time was opportune for a reappraisal of their American policy.

When news of Saratoga reached the chancery in Versailles,[1] the moment of decision arrived. Seeing that Great Britain must now make a desperate effort for reconciliation, or face the prospect of a long, long war, Vergennes wrote: "France must now either support the colonies or abandon them."[2]

Vergennes moved swiftly. He prepared a paper outlining the policy required by new developments. He submitted the paper to Maurepas, the chief minister, and through him Vergennes's new policy went to the king. After consideration by Louis XVI and a Council of State, the resolution to form an alliance with the United States was unanimously adopted on December 12, 1777. A courier left immediately for Spain with the news of Burgoyne's surrender and the French court's decision to make an alliance with the Americans. Vergennes asked the concurrence of the Spanish court as provided for in the Family Compact. When the Spanish court rejected his proposal, France decided to proceed alone.

Burgoyne's surrender brought rejoicing to the Americans at Passy, but Franklin knew a crisis was at hand. He felt that America could play Great Britain against France, and determined to make the most of the situation. Throughout 1777 Franklin's diplomacy had been unaggressive. He believed it in the interest of France to save the American colonies. The loss of England's American commercial monopoly would repay France for supporting American independence. His refusal to "court" France, his reluctance to "bind America beyond its true interests," had been reported in London and perhaps was decisive in the British campaign for reconciliation which followed. William Carmichael thought Franklin trembled "for Fear his Propositions would be accepted in France. He wishes no European Connections."[3]

Saratoga came as a distinct surprise to the British. If 1777 was a year of "watchful waiting" for the French, it had been a year of hope for the English, at least until October. Lord North was considering how to speak of America in the King's Speech to Parliament. To William Eden, Under Secretary of State for Foreign Affairs, he put the question, "How shall we mention America? Shall we be very stout? or shall we take advantage of the flourishing state of our affairs to get out of the d____d war, and hold a moderate language?"[4] News of Burgoyne's surrender arrived on December 2. Lord George Germain, the Secretary of War, wrote Eden that he could think of nothing but America, and asked if Eden "thought of any Expedient for extracting this country out of its distress?"[5] Eden did think of something. With North's approval, but under Eden's supervision, Paul Wentworth, former colonial agent and now a British agent, left two days later in an eleventh-hour attempt to forestall the Franco-American alliance.

Wentworth was only one of several agents who appeared independently and secretly to open negotiations with Franklin. He received instructions from William Eden. The avowed purpose of his mission was to prevent the alliance. The British ministers were prepared to meet all demands of the colonists but independence. Wentworth was to inquire if the colonies, in lieu of taxes, would meet the cost of their government? If charters were restored, would the colonies restore confiscated property? He was to urge normal commerce, with the mutual guarantee of all possessions based upon common citizenship. The letter urged the commissioners to state the areas which they considered negotiable.

The letter was an appeal to the commissioners to consider all issues before making a decision. Eden appealed to national pride, sentiment, common interest. He warned America against an alien nation. He said the war could end to the honor and satisfaction of all if the Americans accepted "qualified control" and did not insist on independence. To show good faith Wentworth was, if necessary, to permit the commissioners to read Eden's letter.

It is likely that the sentiments in another of William Carmichael's intercepted letters guided Eden. Carmichael had said that if the commissioners "could on one side lose the idea of supremacy and on the other side that of independence, they might be friends by Treaty never by Confederacy."[6]

Wentworth did not receive instructions as to how he should advance his mission before leaving London. Probably Eden suggested Deane as a good contact. In July 1777 the British agent in Paris, George Lupton, friendly with Deane, had reported to Eden:

> I cannot help mentioning an observation or expression which Mr. Deane made to me and many others and which has startled me, the friend of America. I breakfasted with him on Monday last at which he observed that it was a pity that Great Britain did not bring about a reconciliation with the colonies, and jointly make war against France, but at the same time he observed twould be necessary to let them support their independence, however I imagine a reconciliation might be brought about on favorable terms.[7]

Wentworth left London on December 10, 1777, arriving in Paris two days later. He wrote Deane for an interview, stating that he would wait in his coach the following morning near the barrier to Passy. Then he would attend an exhibition at the Luxembourg Gallery, and in the evening go to the Pot de Vin Bathing House on the river, leaving a note with the number of his room with the attendant. Wentworth informed Deane that "in the meeting the greatest secrecy and honour is expected."[8] Deane replied he would see anyone who had business with him and would always treat every subject and honor its merit.[9] Wentworth mentioned he was on the point of returning to London "where you may have wishes to make me useful in which I shall be happy if they promote a peace." The two men met at dinner, and after pledging "secrecy and the confidence of private gentlemen wishing well to both countries," they reviewed the antecedents of the conflict without arriving at a common view.

Next morning Wentworth called for Deane at the Cafe St. Honoré, where he was having breakfast with Franklin and Arthur Lee. After the meal the two men went off together to continue the discussion in which Wentworth reported that Deane displayed a great deal of republican pride.

In their second meeting Wentworth outlined his plan for reconciliation, to be based on amnesty and the colonial status at the time of the treaty of 1763. The colonies were to be self-governing. Parliament was to interpose in external affairs. An armistice would enable British troops to withdraw except from New York and neighboring islands. He suggested that American leaders could have such offices as Privy Seal, Great Seal, local baronies, knighthoods, and governor-generalships. He suggested a loan of thirty million pounds for agriculture and sound currency.[10] It was a rosy picture, and Deane showed interest by arranging another meeting.

Deane failed to keep this new appointment. He pleaded illness. Nevertheless, he arranged a meeting between Wentworth and Franklin. Franklin stipulated no mention of personal rewards and that the meeting would have to appear accidental. Doubtless, Deane and Franklin had discussed the previous conversations.

In his *Journal* Arthur Lee described his reaction upon learning of the Deane-Wentworth conversations.

> In the evening Mr. Lee visited Mr. Commissioner Izard, who asked if he had heard anything of a proposal to the Commissioners within a few days from England. Mr. Lee said no. He [Izard] replied, "you are ill treated, and you ought to call Mr. Deane to a severe account for his conduct; for that Paul Wentworth had a meeting with Mr. Deane to whom he made propositions, which Mr. D. gave to the French ministry." Mr. L said that he had not heard one syllable of it; that he would enquire into it; but that being a public wrong, he could not resent it personally.[11]

The next day at noon Arthur Lee went to Passy. Commissioner Lee immediately asked Deane "whether a Mr. Wentworth was in town and whether he had seen him?" Mr. Deane said "that Mr. Wentworth had desired to see him, that he knew little of him, that he expressed a desire for accommodation, and upon what terms it could be obtained, for that he thought the ministry in England were disposed to it. This was all he communicated upon the subject."[12] With the exception of Arthur Lee's feelings, the negotiations were a success. Deane did the work and, having led Wentworth to expect success, he turned the affair over to Franklin. The French ministers were informed of each proposal made by the British agent.

The meeting between Wentworth and Franklin lasted for two hours, and Wentworth read parts of Eden's letter of December 5. Franklin was more noncommittal than Deane. Wentworth proposed to send Deane and Franklin to England under a safe conduct to deal directly with the ministers. Franklin closed the conversation by stating that America would never consent to peace without independence and that he had no power to deal with Great Britain on any basis.[13]

From Paris Wentworth reported to Eden the progress of his mission. Eden immediately forwarded the information to Lord North. The latter commented to Eden: "I was about two hours reading Wentworth's despatches last night. I do not know what to think of them, and I cannot pretend to judge whether there is, or is not any wish of peace in 51 [code name for Deane]."[14] The entire correspondence went to George III with North's comment: "This expedition of Mr. Wentworth's may very possibly end in nothing, but (as he speaks entirely for himself, Lord North hopes and believes that no mischief can arise from it), especially as he had the greatest confidence in the discretion and ability of Mr. Wentworth."[15]

In his diagnosis and evaluation of Wentworth's mission, North was wrong. The astute Franklin had sensed the advantage in each British offer of reconciliation. He seized each opportunity to increase his bargaining power, informing the French ministers of offers made not only by Wentworth but also by other agents who appeared independent of each other. He was silent on the terms. Gérard noted to Vergennes that in conversation Deane "spoke to me with much uneasiness of the conduct of Mr. Hutton, and confessed that Dr. Franklin was very reticent in this matter."[16] Vergennes instructed Gérard to maintain contact with Deane, because "I do not suspect that any reticence exists on the side of our friend." Wentworth was placed under observation, and each visitor noted and reported. Meanwhile, Deane and Franklin had been considering the overtures from Great

Britain, and Vergennes had commissioned Gérard to negotiate with the three American commissioners for an alliance.

Opening negotiations with the American commissioners, Gérard's first step was to invite Deane to Versailles. In his report to Vergennes, Gérard wrote: "I confided my plan to Mr. Deane that, having regard to our previous interviews, I might be commissioned to announce to him the execution of a treaty, but I begged him not to inform his colleagues. This confidence which this Deputy puts in me seemed to require this preliminary disclosure, and his conduct has justified it." Deane refused to hear any proposal unless his colleagues were present, and arranged a meeting of the commissioners with Gérard without disclosing the purpose. The subject for the December 17 meeting was French aid needed to assure American independence.

Gérard requested secrecy concerning the meeting and the subjects discussed. After slight hesitation Franklin broke the silence by saying, "I promise," followed by Lee and Deane. Gérard asked two questions: "1. What would they, the Deputies, consider sufficient to reject all the proposals of England, which did not include recognition of full and absolute independence both in proposals of England, which did not include recognition of full and absolute independence both in politics and trade? and 2. What would they consider equally necessary to produce the same effect on Congress and the American people?" Franklin raised the question of France's entry into the war, but Gérard pointed out that his was a question he was not empowered to discuss. It stood to reason that war would follow, and he knew that the king was prepared, but he could say no more on this subject. Having sidestepped the issue, Gérard wished to withdraw so that the deputies might consider answers to his questions privately.

At the end of an hour Gérard returned and found Franklin writing a reply. At Deane's request, Franklin read their joint answer to the first question. Franklin reviewed the "fruitlessness of their proceedings and the difficulties they had experienced." Finally, he read an article, as Gérard later reported, that conclusion of a treaty of commerce and alliance would induce the American deputies to close their ears to any proposal which should not guarantee their political and commercial independence. Gérard stopped him and stated that the king and his ministers, "having presumed that such would be the desire of the deputies, I have been authorized to tell them that whenever they should judge that treaty necessary His Majesty was resolved to at once conclude it, and that it would be begun as soon as they wished." Franklin returned to France's entry into the war. Gérard hesitated, "but Mr. Deane encouraged me with a glance," and again being pressed by Franklin said two treaties might be concluded— the first of peace, friendship, and commerce; the second, of alliance. The first would recognize the United States and treat her as an equal. Gérard explained that the alliance would depend upon events. The only stipulation the king would make was that the colonists continue war until the British left North America. In his final report of the meeting, Gérard wrote to Vergennes: "I had dwelt on the conquest of the whole continent because Deane had confided to me that this was according to the Doctor's way of thinking, and the most definite reason for forming ties with France, which he was inclined to think the United States could otherwise do without."

At this meeting the Americans learned that Spain had declined to recognize the United States or join the alliance. The disappointment of the Americans, especially Franklin, was acute. "The Doctor after some moments of silence, replied with some emotion: 'We have always been given to understand, and we have always thought that the resolves of France were common to Spain.' "[17]

Gérard submitted to Franklin, Lee, and Deane drafts of the two treaties on January 18, 1778. Two weeks passed in details. In accord with Gérard's former statement that the king of France was "too great, too just and too generous" to gain advantage, he counted "only on the advantages which would result from mutual interest." With regard to France's renunciation of commercial monopolies, Gérard had stated and now proved the king "eager to give to all Europe as well as America on this occasion an example of disinterestedness, by asking of the United States only such things as it might suit them to grant equally to any other power." This commercial treaty with no involvement was what Benjamin Franklin and John Adams as well as Thomas Paine had in mind.

In the second treaty, the Treaty of Alliance, the commissioners faced "political entanglements." This instrument was to come into force only in case of hostilities between Great Britain and France (Article I). Article II declared: "The essential and direct End of the present defensive alliance is to maintain effectually the liberty, Sovereignty, and independence absolute

[54]

and unlimited of the said United States, as well as in Matters of Government as of commerce." Article VI dealt with territorial claims: "The most Christian King renounces forever the possession of the island of Bermudas as well as any part of the continent of North America which before the treaty of Paris in 1763, or in virtue of that Treaty, were acknowledged to belong to the Crown of Great Britain, or the United States heretofore called British Colonies, or which are at this time or have been lately under the Power of the King and Crown of Great Britain." In accord with the wish of the king of France, the Treaty stated that "neither of the two Parties shall conclude either Truce or Peace with Great Britain, without the formal consent of the other first obtain'd; and they mutually engage not to lay down arms, until the Independence of the United States shall have been formally and tacitly assured by the Treaty or Treaties that shall terminate the war."[18]

Negotiation between the French and Americans revealed no basic difference of opinion. Still, a problem developed with Articles XI and XII of the Treaty of Amity and Commerce related to Gérard's proposal that France impose no export duty on molasses purchased by the Americans in the French West Indies, in return for which the United States should place no export duty upon American commodities purchased by Frenchmen. At first Arthur Lee approved, but changed his mind after consulting Ralph Izard of South Carolina, then in Paris as commissioner to the court of Tuscany.[19] Izard, Arthur Lee, and William Lee concluded that Silas Deane, with Franklin's acquiesence, was attempting to favor New England's commercial interests at the expense of southern agriculture.[20] Again Deane acted merely as Franklin's assistant. After the sessions, Deane often went to Versailles in the evening to confer with Gérard. When Arthur Lee was found still dissatisfied with Articles XI and XII of the Treaty of Amity and Commerce, Deane and Franklin agreed to support him.

To this Gérard replied that the king had given assent and any change would require long delay, that Congress would be at liberty to strike the two articles and the French king would not object.

The treaties were signed February 6, 1778. Except for the differences over Articles XI and XII, the American commissioners had worked together harmoniously, if not always happily. Arthur Lee had proposed consulting William Lee and Ralph Izard, commissioners for Berlin-Vienna and Tuscany respectively, but Franklin and Deane demurred on the ground that the two commissioners were not empowered to treat with France. This rejection increased the irritation of Lee and his friends with Deane.

Now, as official envoys, Franklin, Deane, and Lee went to Versailles on (Man) May 20, 1778. They presented their credentials to the king and received all the honor due representatives of a great power. The reception given Franklin by the people of Paris and at the palace demonstrated his popularity. When the envoys' coaches entered the outer courtyard, a military band played, the French flag dipped in official salute, and a Guard of Honor presented arms. As the envoys entered the palace, they met the major of the Swiss Guard who presented them as "Les ambassadeurs des treize provinces unies." The court rose and saluted. When Vergennes noticed that Franklin was suffering from fatigue, he waived formalities and presented the old philosopher to the king. Louis XVI glanced at the credentials and as a mark of honor and esteem engaged the American representative in direct conversation.

The great object of the mission was a reality—the United States of America had become a member of the family of nations. She had acquired an ally and no longer stood alone in the war with Great Britain. To Silas Deane, the merchant from Connecticut, must go a large share of credit for the completion and success of this mission.

CHAPTER 6

DEANE'S RECALL

IN compliance with an order from Congress, Silas Deane, after twenty-two months in France, left Paris on March 31, 1778. James Lovell, the Acting Secretary of the Committee on Foreign Affairs, had written that "the order was complimentary to your abilities of serving these United States and needs no further explanation." Deane suspected more to his recall than a mere report to Congress.[1]

Although aware that he had enemies, Deane resented what he considered censure of his conduct. In early January 1778 he admitted to John Ross that he had been conscious of gathering clouds and had long known that what could be done would be done against him, but said he would never take measures to counteract accusations which would make him appear small in his own eyes.[2] A few days before leaving Deane again expressed his irritation to Ross: "I wish to know what has been the complaint against me, for I have not received one word on the subject from Congress or my particular friends."[3]

Deane's first reaction was to remain in France until Congress informed him of the reason for his recall. Upon Franklin's advice and Beaumarchais's recommendation, he decided to return. He expected somehow to demolish his enemies, vindicate himself, and be back in France by autumn.[4] His departure coincided with a radical change in French foreign policy and a rupture in personal relations between Benjamin Franklin and Arthur Lee

—a break long coming, but precipitated by Deane's departure. Deane was thus a cause of controversies on both sides of the Atlantic.

Normally, the recall of an agent by his government does not concern and certainly does not involve the government to which he is accredited. Deane's recall proved an exception. Vergennes and his cabinet colleagues chose to read into the recall a victory for the antialliance party in Congress. Should the Americans reject the treaties signed by the commissioners, France, now espousing the American cause and with the treaties known to the public, might have to meet Great Britain alone—a prospect she did not desire. Vergennes knew that to block the treaties the new Carlisle Commission in England would make far-reaching concessions to the Americans. The minister, aware of the strong antialliance sentiment in Congress, in a paper prepared for the king, dated January 7, 1778, wrote:

> We are informed that there is a numerous party in which is endeavouring to fix as a basis of the political system of the new States that no engagement be contracted with the European powers. Doctor Franklin himself professes this dogma. Necessity alone has prevented its being established; but as soon as that ceases to exist, the insurgents who will have asserted their independence without our help will think they do not need it in order to maintain their independence. Then we shall be without any bond with them exposed to their avidity and perhaps their resentment.[5]

Therefore, if Deane's recall was a victory for the antialliance forces, Deane as symbol of the Franco-American Alliance must have protection from the common enemy.

In a secret memoir dated March 13, 1778, ten days after learning of the recall, Beaumarchais traced the blame to Arthur Lee. He noted that "Mr. Arthur Lee, from his character and his ambition, at first was jealous of Mr. Deane. He has ended by becoming his enemy, as always happens in little minds more concerned to supplant their rivals than to surpass them in merit." Beaumarchais reasoned that, to accomplish his goal, Lee had rendered Deane "an object of suspicion to Congress." He had exploited the unpopularity and resentments caused by Deane's contracts with foreign officers, and written to his brothers that supplies from Beaumarchais were a gift from the French government. "Thus it is clear, in my opinion that while England sends Commissioners to America, and Mr. Lee's relatives and friends exert themselves to render popular a reconciliation between the two countries, there is at the same time an attempt to destroy by slander the influence or the credit of Mr. Deane and myself—the men known to be the most attached to the policy of an alliance between France and America."

To show their displeasure with Congress in recalling Deane, the French ministers decided to bestow upon him the highest marks of esteem and affection. Again, as in 1776, it was Beaumarchais who recommended the policy to Vergennes. Beaumarchais, realizing that diplomatic activity would soon shift to Philadelphia, persuaded Vergennes to send a minister plenipotentiary to the United States to insure ratification of the treaties. He selected a man who held Silas Deane in high regard—Conrad A. Gérard.

Deane was to accompany the new minister plenipotentiary on the flagship of the French squadron of warships then on its way to American waters. According to Beaumarchais's plan, Deane was to return "loaded with personal honors."[6] In his dispatch case Deane carried a portrait of Louis XVI set in diamonds, a letter from Franklin praising him as a faithful, active, and able servant of the public, and letters of commendation from Ministers Maurepas, Sartine, and Vergennes. The last statesman outdid himself, and praised "the zeal, activity and intelligence with which he has conducted the interests of the United States, by which he has merited the esteem of the King, my master, and for which his Majesty has been pleased to give him marks of his satisfaction."[7]

To Beaumarchais went the task of disillusioning Congress, if need be, that the supplies sent by Rodrigue Hortalez and Company were not a gift from the French government but a legitimate commercial transaction. For the first time, Beaumarchais informed Congress officially that Hortalez and Company and Caron de Beaumarchais were one and the same, explained the origin of secret aid, and exonerated Deane from any wrong:

Although I am known to you, Gentlemen, only by Rodrigue Hortalez, a signature adopted in order to conceal my commercial operations with you up to the present time, my name is Caron de Beaumarchais. Long before the arrival of Mr. Deane in France, I had conceived the plan of founding a business firm sufficiently strong and devoted to incur the risques of the sea and of a war, in carrying to you, as I was informed, for the equipment of your troops. I spoke to Mr. Arthur Lee at London, of this project, and not only asked whether he had any method of securing commercial intercourse between us, but I also wrote him from France that if he could assure me of the prompt arrival of return, in the products of your country, to pay for my shipments and furnish me anew with the means of serving you, I might perhaps arouse the interest of some exceedingly wealthy friends of mine and obtain their assistance. Mr. Lee replied that if I insisted upon prompt payments in tobacco, these operations would be considerably drawn out, and he besought me to continue sending stores and supplies in the interval. I answered that having applied to the authorities themselves for their clandestine support, in the shape of material advances, and having been refused, I should merely form a trading company to cooperate with me, in sending shipments, conditional upon the speediest possible returns from America.

Since Mr. Lee did not reply to my letter, I was endeavoring alone to found this Company when Mr. Deane came to France. From the moment of his arrival, I corresponded with no one else.[8]

One unexpected result of Deane's recall was the explosion in relations between Benjamin Franklin and Arthur Lee. The exact time when Lee learned of Deane's recall and his immediate reaction is unknown. On March 18, 1778, Lee's friend, the Comte de Lauraguais, informed Louis XVI's chief minister, Maurepas, that Lee had told him of Deane's recall. Lee did not know that Deane had left the city until after he had gone. Nor did he learn of Gérard's appointment until a few hours before Gérard left Paris —then only because Gérard called and spoke of the appointment. The extent of Lee's information and what he planned to make of it are difficult to ascertain. If he looked for an opportunity to reflect upon Deane's public and personal honesty, the situation was ready-made. He could suggest that Deane's hurry to leave France was a deliberate attempt to avoid settling accounts. Although the suggestion was plausible to the casual observer and many members of Congress, Deane's letter of March 29 to Beaumarchais provided counterevidence: "It is unhappy that the short time allowed me to prepare for my voyage will not admit of our making at least a general settlement of your accounts; but the absolute necessity of my setting out immediately, obliges me to leave my other transactions in the same unsettled state."[9]

On March 31, the day Deane left Paris, Arthur Lee wrote a joint letter to Deane and Franklin, touching off an epistolary exchange. These letters revealed Lee's resentment, frustration, and determination to control the Paris mission. He wrote of rumors that Deane would be leaving Paris and repeated the "request that I long ago and repeatedly made, that we should settle accounts" immediately because most of the vouchers were in Deane's possession.[10]

Franklin, a mild, easygoing man, was inclined to see the best in everyone. On March 31 he had written a complimentary letter to Congress regarding Silas Deane. On April 1 he revealed to Arthur Lee that when duly provoked he could and would use plain language. "There is a style in some of your letters, I observe it particularly in the last, whereby superior merit is assumed to yourself in point of care and attention to business and blame is insinuated on your colleagues without making yourself accountable, by a direct charge of negligence or unfaithfulness, which has the appearance of being as artful as it is unkind. In the present case I think that the insinuation is groundless." Franklin denied that either Deane or he had been unwilling to settle accounts prior to Deane's departure. The banker's book contained "the whole," and Lee "who had abundantly more leisure" could have examined the accounts and asked for an explanation. "You never did either." As Deane had left "both the public papers and explications," it was easy to settle accounts. "You have only to name the day and place, and I will attend the business with you."[11]

The second round of the Franklin-Lee imbroglio occurred immediately. On April 2 Lee accused Franklin of concealing the date of Deane's departure. This was true. Lee did not know, and Franklin did not feel free to say, that Vergennes had requested that both he and Deane keep the secret from their colleague. Vergennes had learned that Lee's private secretary, Thornton, in London on a mission, had been using official information for stock-jobbing. Vergennes was apprehensive that if Lee knew the sailing date of the French fleet this information would reach London by the same channel. Lee later discovered that Thornton was in the pay of Lord North and discharged him. Franklin, instead of telling Lee of the suspicion attached to his secretary, merely replied that Deane had been asked to keep the secret and that he had complied.

In the same letter Lee expressed indignation that Gérard had been appointed minister without consulting him. Franklin pointed out that the French had made the decision. "Your angry charge, therefore, or our 'making a party business of it' is groundless. We had no hand in the business."

In his letter of April 1 Franklin had requested Lee to set the date for an examination of the public accounts, but Lee once again, on April 2, charged that his request to settle accounts had been ignored. Franklin replied sharply: "When this comes to be read in Committee, for whom it seems to be calculated rather than for me, who knows the circumstances, what can they understand by it, but that you are the only careful, honest man of the three, and that we have some knavish reason for keeping the accounts in the dark and you from seeing the vouchers?" The truth was, as Lee knew, that the papers were kept at Passy because Franklin and Deane lived there, and had conducted most of the business because Lee had been gone on long journeys. "I never knew that you desired to have the keeping of them. You were never refused a paper, or a copy of a paper that you desired."[12]

In the same style Franklin told Lee he had served many causes in his long life and "there is not a single instance of my ever being accused before of acting contrary to their interest or my duty." He reminded Lee that he was accountable to Congress. "I saw your jealous, suspicious, malignant, and quarrelsome temper, which was daily manifesting itself against Mr. Deane and almost every other person you had any concern with. I therefore passed your affronts in silence, did not answer but burnt your angry letters, and received you when I next saw you, with the same civility as if you had never wrote them."[13]

In a more characteristic vein, Franklin wrote to his old friend in Philadelphia, Francis Hopkinson: "At present I do not know of more than two enemies that I enjoy, viz., Lee and Izard. I deserve the enmity of the latter, because I might have avoided it by paying him a compliment, which I neglected. That of the former I owe to the people of France, who happened to respect me too much and him too little—which I could bear, and he could not."[14]

Arthur Lee continued to pour his suspicion and grievances into the ears of a Congress which "did not understand the circumstances." Deane's replacement, John Adams, soon found it difficult to maintain a neutral position in the commission. He was falsely accused of joining forces with Arthur Lee. The Lees in America had helped select Adams with a plan in mind.[15] The Lees in France had been coached how to handle him.[16]

To friends and enemies alike, Adams's evaluation of Deane's conduct and services was the same. Adams justified his reputation for frankness in a letter to William McCreary, an old friend in America: "I have never been used to disguise my sentiments of Men whom I have been against in public life and I certainly should not begin with Mr. Deane, who is not and never was a man of importance to make me deviate from a rule I have observed all my life . . . and if I had been against Mr. Deane I should certainly avow it and make no secret of it at all."[17] To James Lovell, no friend of Deane's, Adams wrote that he had heard "great panegyrics and harsh censure" regarding Deane. "But I believe he has neither the merit that some persons ascribe to him, nor the gross faults to answer for which others impute or suspect. I believe he was a diligent servant of the public and rendered it useful service."[18]

Adams was equally explicit in an August letter to Richard Henry Lee. For his friend and colleague Arthur Lee he had genuine liking. In regard to Deane he was no less emphatic: "I will have nothing to do with design and endeavors to run down characters, to paint in odious colors in different action, to excite or propagate suspicions without evidence, or to foment or entertain prejudices of any kind, if I can possibly avoid it."[19]

Many Lee partisans urged that Adams could and should tell Congress "the truth." But if John Adams had anything to say against Deane, he never said it. His silence is good reason to believe that he did not change the views he expressed to William McCreary, James Lovell, and Richard Henry Lee.

Meanwhile the Lees were busy. The private correspondence of the Lee brothers and their associates shows they had cultivated congressional displeasure with Deane. Ralph Izard, the American commissioner to Tuscany, wrote in November 1777 to John Lloyd, an American merchant, South Carolina politician, and friend of both Izard and the Lees: "I am confident your idea of a man [Deane] is just in every particular, but our opinions concerning him, as also others, it will be most prudent to reserve solely to ourselves, for reasons which are sufficiently manifest."[20] In his reply, Lloyd stated:

I am told that the brothers of the gentlemen whom you have just mentioned are leading members of Congress, and that they have in consequence great influence. If that is the case, I think Deane stands on very uncertain ground, as you may depend upon it his conduct will not be represented in the most favourable point of view by them, which joined M[orris]'s inveteracy, will form a collective power that may throw him from his present exalted pinnacle to the dreadful abyss of native insignificance. From the intimations of a friend of Deane's I have some cause to believe that such an event would not be unexpected.[21]

Unlike their brother Arthur, William and Richard Henry Lee were too astute to make rash charges against Deane. William counseled care to his brothers on both sides of the Atlantic. In early January 1778 William cautioned Richard Henry Lee "with respect to charges against Mr. Deane and Mr. Carmichael I think you should weigh the matter with Loudoun [Francis Lightfoot] very cautiously and only move when you see the way very clear."[22] William Lee wrote Arthur in April: "I think great caution ought to be used . . . with Deane . . . [but] if anything decisive can be got at, no time should be lost in conveying it."[23]

The influence of the Lee brothers on Deane's recall is difficult to determine from letters by Arthur and William Lee to their brothers in Congress. It is true that Richard Henry Lee defended Deane's "distressing contracts" to Samuel Adams, yet it was the same Richard Henry Lee who in Congress moved recall because it "would have been out of character to continue him."[24] This is a curious comment.

Sending French officers to America was a great source of resentment and certainly worked against Deane. In the correspondence of the Secretary of the Secret Committee, James Lovell, this antagonism was apparent. In December 1777 Franklin informed Lovell that "you have no conception of how we are still besieged . . . by personal application" from French officers. "I hope, therefore, that favorable allowance will be made to my worthy colleague on account of his situation at the time, as he has long since corrected that mistake and daily approves himself, to my certain knowledge, an able, faithful, active and extremely useful servant of the public; a testimony I think it is my duty to take this occasion to giving to his merit not asked, as, considering my great age, I may probably not live to give it personally in Congress, and I perceive he has enemies."[25] Franklin assured

Lovell in July that the commissioners had never received instructions regarding the employment of foreign officers. "You mention former letters of the committee, by which we might have seen the apprehension of the resentment, etc. Those letters never came to hand. And we, on our part, are amazed to hear that the committee had no line from us for near a year, during which we had written, I believe, five or six long and particular letters . . ."26

It is certain that Lovell, the self-styled "Mr. Secretary" of the Secret Committee of Correspondence, questioned Deane's fitness for office. In June 1777 he wrote to Joseph Trumbull of Connecticut: "I have but a poor Ideal of that Gentleman's ability to guard against french [sic] finesse and flattery."27 And to General William Whipple, congressional delegate from New Hampshire, in the same month Lovell expressed the same opinion, "it appears that Deane is only a child in the hands of Du Coudray."28 Deane's former colleague from Connecticut in the First and Second Continental Congresses, Eliphalet Dyer, wrote to Trumbull: "This is a most unhappy affair [Du Coudray] and our old Friend D[e]ane has been in more Instances than one, Imprudent to the last degree."29 Lovell informed General Washington in July that bad as was Du Coudray's contract, Franklin had eliminated the worst features from the one made by Deane.

In July 1777 the idea that a recall was necessary appeared for the first time in Lovell's extensive correspondence. To James Whipple he wrote: "Ought not this weak or roguish [sic] man be recalled; if as a corresponding Agent he did this, what will not he think himself entitled to do as a commissioner!"30 Henry Laurens of South Carolina, an honest man but devoted to the Lees, complained in August that the "late flood of French Men rushed in upon us under agreements with Mr. Deane has reduced Congress to a painful dilemma."31 The same month Laurens observed to John Rutledge of South Carolina, "one of our agents [obviously Deane] has not discovered competency to the immense work in hand."32 Lovell wrote to Oliver Wolcott of Connecticut in August: "If Silas and his connekions [sic] could have a good opening to transfer their whole property to the other side of the water, it is not impossible that they would gladly do it."33

Then the blow fell. On September 8, 1777, Congress repudiated Deane's contracts with all foreign officers, on the grounds "that Mr. Deane had no authority to make such conventions, and that Congress therefore are not bound to ratify or fulfill them." Richard Henry Lee moved on November 21, 1777, and Congress "resolved that Silas Deane be recalled from the court of France."[34] William Williams described the vote to Trumbull:

the motion, made last July was revived for recalling Mr. Deane, was again taken up and carried without a dissenting Voice. He died at last very easie, tho there had been at sund. [sic] Times before, the most violent and convulsive throes and Exertions on the same Question. . . . A motion is also made that it be left to the remaining Commiss. to Judge on the Spot, wethr. Mr. Deane may not yet be employed at some other Court, the Motion dropd, and I trust will never be carried.[35]

Lovell described the last chapter of the recall in a letter to Richard Henry Lee: "The day after you left York, I moved Congress for an order in the following words. 'Whereas it is of the greatest Importance the Congress should, at this critical conjuncture be well informed of the State of Affairs in Europe, and whereas Congress has resolved that the Honble. Silas Deane Esqr. be recalled . . . and direct him to embrace the first opportunity of returning to America and upon his arrival to repair with all possible dispatch to Congress."[36] On the same day he wrote Deane: "The order stands in need of no comment from the committee to elucidate it; and being drawn up in terms complimentary to your abilities of serving these United States . . ."[37]

Rumors about Deane's recall were widespread. A British spy in Paris, George Lupton, reported to London in September 1777 that Thomas Morris gave out that Deane was to be recalled, and Carmichael told Lupton he imagined Deane would leave his present employment and receive another of less consequence.[39] Beaumarchais's agent in Philadelphia, De Francey, wrote in December 1777 that Deane had been recalled and was a very ill-used man.

Thus, it is possible Deane was a victim of congressional disfavor because of lack of communication. The letters of James Lovell and others of the Lee supporters indicate, however, that hints suggesting Deane's recall had been placed with influential people.

The exact reason or reasons for Silas Deane's recall may perhaps never be known. Richard Henry Lee, author of the motion of recall, insisted that the reasoning be omitted from the *Journals of Congress*.[38] Congress lacked the courage to make an explanation to Deane.

CHAPTER 7

DEANE AND CONGRESS

GREAT events had occurred in the United States in the twenty-two months Silas Deane had been in France: the Americans had declared their independence, an entire British army had surrendered, and France had become the ally of the new nation. These tremendous accomplishments accompanied a disastrous currency inflation, a general war-weariness, and return of many of the original congressional revolutionary leaders to positions in state government or other nonfederal assignments. The loss of these men from the legislative council of the nation naturally meant a decline in the prestige of Congress—a loss the young nation could ill afford.

During the early years of the Revolution, while the insurgent colonies were fighting with little success for what they considered their rights, many patriots attempted to sidestep factional differences for the sake of the common cause. But the Conway Cabal in 1777 brought personal and sectional differences into the open. Although the Cabal's attempt to remove Washington from command came to nothing, Congress suffered a great loss of prestige in the aftermath. The year 1778 was the nadir of congressional unpopularity and of partisan strife. Titus Hosmer described conditions in a report to Connecticut Governor Trumbull on August 31, 1778, deploring that Congress had no power to compel delegates to attend sessions. They seldom assembled before eleven o'clock. Several members were adept at raising questions of order, starting debate upon trifling amendments, and generally wasting time, leaving the public business undone. Hosmer found it disturbing that the old prejudices of North against South were reviving, and this trouble was compounded by delegates who wanted to break the union and destroy independence.

Silas Deane's return sparked the explosion of these factional and sectional differences. The alliance in Congress between the Virginia Lees and the Massachusetts Adamses cut through the natural dissensions between North and South. A personal element appeared in this coalition which represented primarily an alliance of agricultural forces against commercial interests. Robert Morris led the Eastern mercantile interests, and Richard Henry Lee and Samuel Adams the opposing faction. Broadly speaking, Deane was supported by the mercantile interest and opposed by the agricultural group. The feud between Arthur Lee and Deane only increased the trouble.

Deane's recall had been the work of Richard Henry Lee, but it is impossible to prove the existence of a plot to get Deane. It is true that R. H. Lee rejoiced over Deane's recall and assured Arthur that "Deane, as well as others, shall be attended to here."[1] Letters from William to Richard Henry Lee contain the policy, "not to let any of his accounts for the expenditure of public money finally pass without the most authentic vouchers."[2]

Deane later maintained that a friend, whom he did not identify, told him soon after his arrival that there were those who wished to sacrifice him to his enemies, to wear him out by delays, to ruin him by insinuation, hint, and innuendo. Although he might rely on the justice of Congress, his enemies would take measures to delay it in a way that would prove prejudicial if not ruinous to him.[3]

Controversy and suspicion, then, if not a plot, was the political climate in America when the French fleet dropped anchor in Delaware Bay on July 9, 1778.

The arrival of the French Minister Plenipotentiary opened another chapter in the history of the young nation. Deane immediately notified President Henry Laurens that the French fleet and Minister Gérard had arrived.[4] On July 14, accompanied by a congressional committee, Gérard proceeded to Philadelphia where he took temporary lodging in the house of General Benedict Arnold, the Commandant of the city.

Congress now faced the problem of how to receive a Minister Plenipotentiary. After much debate Congress received the first accredited foreign representative. In honor of the event each member of Congress brought two guests to the formal reception. The sentiments expressed by Gérard in his prepared address and President Laurens's reply met general approval.

If the big news of the moment was Minister Gérard's arrival and reception, Silas Deane's return did not pass without press comment.[5] A slight illness prevented Deane from accompanying Gérard to Philadelphia. When he finally arrived, old friends welcomed him warmly and members of Congress were cordial. During the minister's reception Deane waited quietly for Congress to find time to receive him. Twenty days after his return, he tactfully reminded President Laurens that he awaited the pleasure of Congress.[6]

General George Washington soon wrote Deane expressing appreciation for service to the revolutionary cause. Deane replied, saying how happy he was to find his conduct had met with the general's approval. He mentioned that friends had told him the reason for his recall. The letter did not reveal bitterness, but pointed out that, in haste to comply with orders of Congress, he had left his affairs unsettled and had to return to France in either a private or public capacity to attend to them.[7]

Deane appeared before Congress on August 14, 1778. It became apparent that he had not been summoned home to report on European affairs, although James Lovell's letter accompanying the recall stated he was to make such a report. There was reason to think that his enemies, having accomplished recall, were willing to mark the case closed. When Deane presented himself to Congress, he was introduced and seated at a table on the president's right. He delivered two letters from Franklin and Beaumarchais, which were read and tabled.

When he began his report to Congress, Deane encountered an immediate motion that he present a written report. He withdrew. After a long debate, the motion lost. The hour of adjournment being near, he was to appear the following Monday to give from memory a general account of his transactions in France. On August 17 Deane reported as ordered. Having made "some progress, he was ordered to withdraw" without apparent reason. Four days later he finished his report and again had to withdraw.

For eighteen more days Deane awaited the pleasure of Congress. He expected that body to inform him if further attendance were necessary. He wrote President Laurens for information. Recognizing that Congress had many problems, he asked if he should make "further attendance." On

September 11 he expressed appreciation to the president for placing his letter before Congress and stated his intention of visiting friends before returning to France.

For two months after mid-July 1778 Deane complied with congressional requests without sign of irritation or reproach. On September 14 he wrote his old friend, John Hancock, a former president of Congress, expressing resentment of his treatment by Congress and placing blame on a "certain triumvirate" whose motives were more personal than patriotic. One he identified by the "baseness and ingratitude" Hancock had received from him; the second as his old colleague, "Roger the Jesuit" Sherman, who with his southern associates had been indefatigably against him since his return to America. The third "rogue" he left unidentified. If the good people of the nation knew how their representatives conducted their business, he wrote, they would not tolerate such ingratitude as he had experienced.[8]

On September 16 Deane received an order to appear before Congress for questioning. The following day, however, a committee reported on letters dated January 5, 6, and 31 from Arthur Lee and letters of January 1778 from Benjamin Franklin and Silas Deane. Richard Henry Lee then informed Congress that William Carmichael, while in France, had publicly charged Deane with misapplication of public money. Congress ordered Lee to submit information in writing. The paper he submitted contained the following charges: (1) Deane misapplied public money, and William Carmichael had protested Deane's conduct; (2) a break had occurred between Lee and the "gentlemen of Passy" because the French ministers had requested Lee's exclusion from the business of the commission. The French request came because of insinuation by Deane; Carmichael upon return to America promised to "fully unfold" the reasons for Deane's conduct toward Lee and rascally "measures he [Deane] had pursued in his public character."[9]

Having been denied access to Congress on September 18, the day he was supposed to report, Deane wrote Congress reviewing the recall and stressing why he had departed hastily from France without closing the accounts and securing vouchers. He was unable to give a detailed report until he had closed all the accounts, he said. Eagerness to settle accounts and secure vouchers was the reason he must return to France. He sent two accounts from the commissioners' Paris banker, Grand, showing expenditure of money to the day of his departure from Paris.[10]

Richard Henry Lee's charge concerning the honesty of a public official was too serious to avoid. Congress decided to examine William Carmichael "touching the said commissioners and the conduct of said commissioners." It postponed reading Deane's letter until Carmichael's examination. The same day Congress ordered Deane to have copies of Ralph Izard's letters reflecting on his character and conduct. Deane later received a copy of Arthur Lee's derogatory letter of June 1, 1778.

William Carmichael's examination began on September 28 and continued through October 5. To those persons who expected sensational disclosures the examination was a failure. It dealt with two incidents: the fitting of two privateers for a cruise in the Mediterranean, and the capture of the Harwick mail packet. Carmichael's answers consisted of such weak rejoinders as "I apprehended," "I thought," and "I assumed."

The critical and last question of the first day dealt with the Mediterranean cruise. The colloquy went as follows:

Q: From the knowledge you had of Mr. Deane's transactions, do you recollect any instance which you apprehend to be a misapplication of the public money?
A: I beg to know whether I am to answer from my own knowledge, or suppositions, or opinions in my own mind?

By a nine-to-two vote Congress decided that hearsay evidence was admissible. When the hearing resumed, Carmichael, again asked if he had heard of any misuse of public money, answered, "I do." Upon being pressed, he faltered:

Q: Did you understand . . . that Mr. Deane was to have been concerned in his private capacity?
A: I did not receive such information as to induce me to believe that he was concerned.
Q: If you did not believe that Mr. Deane was concerned in his private capacity in those vessels, what did you mean when you said that you apprehended the public money was applied to private purposes in that instance?
A: I meant that I thought Mr. Deane applied the public money to supply the deficiency of the money that others were to have advance, but did not, towards the purpose of fitting out these vessels.

The second query dealt with Hodge and the capture of the Harwick packet.

Q: Had you reason to suppose that Mr. Deane was concerned, or any of the Commissioners?
A: I did apprehend at the time that Mr. Deane was concerned in the first equipment.
Q: What reasons induced you to apprehend that Mr. Deane was concerned in the first equipment?
A: I cannot recollect the reasons that induced that belief, but I know that I did at the time apprehend he was concerned.[11]

On October 7 Deane, still not hearing from Congress, requested an "audience" to answer Izard's charges. Congress ordered the letter to lie on the table. On October 12 Deane repeated his request, adding that he planned to return to France next month.[12] In a separate letter he answered Izard's charges. He divided them into one general charge and two specific ones. In response to the contention that it would have been impossible to find a person more unfit than himself for the trust, Deane said that Congress and not Izard should determine his competency. In regard to the first charge of hauteur and presumption in his business transactions, Deane denied business relations with Izard and appealed from this opinion to persons with whom he did have transactions. To the accusation that he had opened dispatches and letters sent by Arthur Lee, he replied that he was surprised Lee had never mentioned the matter to him.

Izard made charges against both Deane and Franklin. He claimed they had deliberately concealed from him opportunities for writing to Congress. Deane asked why he did not include Arthur Lee in this charge, and admitted the commissioners had not considered themselves free "to communicate the treaty or its contents, to anyone until the French Court should consent." They were "in the same situation as to the appointment of Monsieur Gérard and the sailing of the Toulon fleet. As Mr. Lee sent letters by M. Gérard, he must be guilty also."

Deane admitted dissension among the commissioners, but denied that the public interest suffered. The source of hostility among the commissioners was the inclusion in the commercial treaty of Articles XI and XII which provided for an exchange of goods between the French West Indies and the

[73]

United States. Gérard had originated the proposal, which was accepted by all three commissioners. Deane said Arthur Lee changed his mind after conferring with William Lee and Ralph Izard. The three decided that Deane and Franklin were favoring northern commercial interests at the South's expense. An agreement between the commissioners, the court of France, and Gérard resolved the matter: Congress would determine whether or not the two articles would be accepted.

Deane recapitulated the entire William Lee-Thomas Morris story. He explained that the commissioner's acts were based on Thomas Morris's "irregularities," and ended by saying that when Franklin and Deane offered to return the privateering business to William Lee, Commissioner Arthur Lee had refused to sign the letter. In fact, he would not permit it to go out.

To Izard's complaint that it was a high insult to Congress for Deane and Franklin to let Gérard go without giving Izard the least intimation of it, Deane observed that "It was not in his power to permit or prevent nor to communicate it to anyone."

To Izard's apprehension that Deane should return to Europe in some official capacity, Deane maintained he had never "solicited for any appointment" from Congress and had no intention of doing so.[13]

On the same day, October 12, Deane wrote Congress concerning Arthur Lee's charge that he should have settled certain accounts before he left France. He said the contract dated back to September 1777, and dealt with the delivery of goods to American ports. Orders from the French court halting shipment of supplies further complicated the matter. Moreover, Arthur Lee had held up settlement of the contract. When the commission was formed in December 1776, Deane and Franklin requested Chaumont to determine a fair settlement. At first Chaumont declined, saying he "found Mr. Lee of so jealous and unquiet disposition, and so much disposed to abuse everyone that he had any concern with, that he had well-nigh resolved never again to have anything to do with the Commission while he was one of them." Later he had agreed to determine a fair settlement if Lee desired him to undertake the task. "This put off the settlement for the time."[14] Lee had written: "It is this sort of neglect and studied confusion that has prevented Mr. Adams and myself, after a tedious examination of the papers left with Dr. Franklin, from getting any satisfaction as to the expenditure of the public money. All we can find is, that millions have been expended, and almost everything remains to be paid for." Citing the account of Grand, the banker, Deane responded: "The amount of expenditures until the time of my leaving Paris, was 4,046,988.17 livres, and it appears as well, from the nature of the accounts . . . and the explanation in his hands up to the very day I set out from Paris. The particular application, indeed, of every part, could not be known until the several accounts should be given in. Mr. Lee himself signed the orders for much the greater part of the monies."

To Arthur Lee's charge that "almost everything remains to be paid for," Deane replied: "I really know not what he means. Things once paid for are not to be paid for a second time, and the payments stated above are proved by Mr. Grand's account, to have been bona fide made." To Lee's pointed allegation that his name was not on the contracts, Deane said they had been signed when Lee was in Berlin. He had concealed nothing from Lee. As soon as Lee returned from Berlin, he "was made acquainted with the contracts; Messrs. Holker (now in Boston), Sabbatier and Desprez repeatedly conferred with Mr. Lee on the subject in my presence, and when they brought in their accounts, Mr. Lee assisted in adjusting them, and signed with us the order for payment, as Mr. Grand's account and the orders and accounts themselves will show."[15]

On October 14, 1778, Congress ordered Deane's letter of October 12 read, and copies sent to Izard and Arthur Lee in Paris. On November 1 Deane sent Congress plans for an American bank and a fleet. These communications Congress ordered read and laid on the table. On November 19 Deane wrote Congress: "Nothing would give me greater satisfaction than to learn by what part of my public conduct I have merited the neglect which my letters and most respectful solicitations, for months past, to be heard from Congress, have been treated?" Congress received and read this letter on November 20, without comment.[16]

His patience exhausted, Deane considered a more radical move. To his brother Barnabas he confided his plans to lay his case before the public. He was going to visit Bethlehem, Pennsylvania, with Gérard and would start publication of his case "next Thursday." "I have heretofore delayed it, hoping I should not be put to the disagreeable Necessity, and knowing the Effects it must have on public affairs, but the Law of Self defence being the first of all I shall no longer be silent."[17] Since Congress had not replied to his first ten letters, Deane wrote once more on November 30. After this epistle was read on December 1, Congress resolved "That after tomorrow Congress will meet two hours at least each evening, beginning at six o'clock, Saturday evening excepted, until the present state of our foreign affairs shall be fully considered."[18]

President Laurens informed Deane of this decision. Deane thanked Laurens, but noted the omission of a fixed time for his attendance, saying his detention was extremely prejudicial to his private affairs.[19] The same day, the "Address of Silas Deane to the Free and Virtuous Citizens of America" appeared in the *Pennsylvania Packet*. It contained a slashing attack on the Lees, and marked the beginning of a newspaper feud that raged for months and smoldered for years.

In spite of his admission to Barnabas of the need for self-defense, Deane now stated his appeal was for the public good. He was not willing to see an individual or a family "raised upon the ruins of the general weal." The appeal had been necessary because the ears of Congress "have been shut against me. While it was safe to be silent, my lips were closed."

The second part of the "Address" was a review of the commission's work in which Deane said he had been honored with one colleague and saddled with another. He reviewed Arthur Lee's travels in the spring and summer of 1777, and retold the story of the Nantes affair. A new note appeared: Arthur Lee had been suspected of revealing secrets to his one-time friend, the Earl of Shelburne. "The suspicions, whether well or ill founded, were frequently related and urged to Dr. Franklin and myself," Deane said, "and joined to his undisguised hatred of, and expressions of contempt for, the French nation in general, embarrassed us exceedingly, and was of no small prejudice to your affairs."

A more serious charge against Arthur Lee concerned his correspondence with Dr. John Berkenhout, who "had the confidence of the British ministry." Deane accused Lee of giving Berkenhout a letter of introduction to Richard Henry Lee, who had sponsored him when he was suspected as an agent of the British government in America.

Deane charged Arthur Lee with opposing the French treaty. Lee had been "dragged into the treaty with reluctance," and the "continued bickering" over Articles XI and XII had been to gain time for a counterproposal by the British.

Deane listed the offices held by William Lee, and intimated that before Burgoyne's surrender William Lee had been careful to do nothing to prevent retaining the aldermanship in London.

Deane included an account of his recall. He related how he had "placed your papers [Congress] and mine, in safety" and returned to America with all possible haste, and how Congress had delayed hearing him. While denying "pique" against any of the Lee brothers, he justified his appeal to the people.[20]

The publication of Deane's "Address" produced immediate reaction, favorable and unfavorable. Deane again wrote Barnabas: "It has been proposed in the most respectable companies to have the public thanks of the citizens given me for my publication."[21] But the Lee family and supporters reacted promptly. In the *Pennsylvania Packet* of December 8, 1778, Francis Lightfoot Lee requested the public to suspend judgment until after a full investigation. Next day Deane inserted a card in the *Packet* stating that since Congress had resolved to hear him he could not with propriety continue his narrative.

Deane's appeal to the people made Congress a center of conflict. His opponents denounced the publication as an insult to Congress, while his friends saw the appeal as a much-wronged man's attempt to defend his character. Henry Laurens wrote a friend in South Carolina:

This appeal to the people, this rash unnecessary appeal I trust will this day be attended to in Congress, but as I am concerned in no intrigue or Cabal, I am consequently ignorant of the designs of my fellow labourers. The honor and interests of these United States call upon every Delegate in Congress for support. If therefore other men are silent, I will deliver my sentiments on this very extraordinary circumstance and I have in prospect the production of much good out of this evil.[22]

When Congress convened, Laurens laid before the House "information . . . from citizens of respectable characters—that Deane's letter had created anxieties in the minds of good people of this city, and excited tumults among them." He had found the letter "highly derogatory to the honor and interests of these United States," and cited Deane's intention of following the appeal to the people with "a course of letters." He considered it "dishonorable to Congress" to hear Deane that evening as planned, and moved that a committee be appointed to report upon the letters. A motion to read the "Address" in Congress lost by vote of six states to five, for everyone had read the narrative. Laurens's motion accomplished nothing except to order Deane to report to Congress in writing upon his work in Europe. Laurens immediately resigned, and John Jay was elected president of Congress. Jay's election was interpreted as a victory for the pro-Deane forces in Congress.[23]

James Lovell wrote Richard Henry Lee, bringing that protagonist up to date on the affairs of Congress. He noted that Deane "had made himself a culprit before our bar, by refusing to answer any interrogations 'tending to criminate himself.' He was the cause of often delay."[24]

In Paris on December 13, 1778, long before he could have learned of the public appeal of December 5, Arthur Lee wrote Theodoric Bland a letter describing his version of the treaty negotiations in Paris which differed somewhat as to roles played by the different commissioners during the negotiations. He accused Deane of taking credit for the accomplishments of the Paris commission and of organizing a clique against him in America. Lee stated that he did not resent the personal attacks, but assured his friend that it was he, Arthur Lee, who in spite of his colleagues' objections, had insisted that France must officially recognize American sovereignty and independence in the treaty. Articles XI and XII had been inserted in the treaty in spite of his objections, and Congress had agreed with his judgment by deleting the two unacceptable articles from the treaty. In his opinion, Lee felt that Deane and Franklin should have been content with equal praise "when in truth their conduct merited censure." Lee expressed the opinion that some day he might be forced to supply Congress and the public with proof "of these things." He concluded with the accusation, "Mr. Deane is universally understood to have made £60,000 sterling while he was a Commissioner."[25]

The newspaper battle continued. In the *Pennsylvania Packet* of December 15, 1778, "Senex" expressed willingness to follow Francis Lightfoot Lee's suggestion to suspend judgment on Deane's publication. He had expected that some of Lee's friends or connections would attempt to disprove some of the alleged facts. As they corresponded with both of the Lees abroad, "they must have it in their power to satisfy the public mind . . . without delay." Was Arthur Lee commissioner for both France and Spain? Was he intimately acquainted with Dr. Berkenhout and had he given him letters of introduction to Richard Henry Lee? Was William Lee commissioner for both Vienna and Berlin, and commercial agent for Congress in Europe? Was he alderman of the city of London? Did William Lee charge five percent commission when Williams had charged two percent? "Senex" also felt the Lee brothers held too many offices: "I pretend not to enter into the merits of Messieurs Lees' characters, or to peep behind the curtain; but surely it behooves us to guard against such dangerous precedents."[26]

"Senex" commented approvingly upon the publication of Deane's "Address." He did not believe Deane had intended disrespect, or that Congress so interpreted it. His own friends, in spite of his infirmities, had urged him "to go with them to find out Mr. Deane and express our thanks for his watchful care over the public weal." The public in general, he said, had approved.

A champion on the Lee side was Thomas Paine, author of *Common Sense* and now Secretary of the Committee for Foreign Affairs, whose reply to Silas Deane appeared in the *Pennsylvania Packet* December 15, under the name "Common Sense." The first paragraph by the famous controversialist announced: "I am no stranger to, his negotiations and contracts in France, his differences with his colleagues, the reason of his return to America, and the matters which have occurred since." He chided Deane for alarming the public mind, and declared he was "particularly circumstanced" as "two of the gentlemen he so freely censures are three thousand miles off, and the other two he so freely affronts are members of Congress . . . and however painful may be their feeling, they must attend the progressive conduct of the hour." Paine pointed out that Deane should have known his recall was censure by a body too polite to say so. The phrase "my papers and yours" emphasized "the intricacy of Mr. Deane's own official affairs." Paine asked why Deane endeavored to lead the public's attention to a wrong object and to bury the real reasons, under a tumult of new and perhaps unnecessary suspicions? He ridiculed Deane's statement that the ears of Congress were "shut against me." He took Deane to task for publishing his "Address" just before Congress was to hear him.

Turning to Deane's account of the activities of Arthur and William Lee, which had been characterized as "stubborn and undeniable facts," Paine pointed out that "deductions from them are hypothetical and inconclusive." Such charges against Arthur Lee, William Lee, and Colonel Richard Lee, "whom I have been well acquainted with for three years past, . . . are to me circumstantial evidences of Mr. Deane's unfitness for a public character." Paine commended Arthur Lee for contacts with the Whigs in England, and felt William Lee's retention of office as alderman proof that the people of London were "very good Whigs." Deane's entire appeal he characterized as "a barbarous, unmanly, and unsupported attack on absent characters . . . far superior to his own." Arthur Lee was too much of a gentleman to be uncivil to the French nation and "might with great justice complain against Mr. Deane's contracts." "Common Sense" concluded: "Upon the whole, I cannot help considering this publication as one of the most irrational performances I ever met with."[27]

Paine had meant his last remark to apply to Deane's "Address," but there were those who felt it should apply to his own remarks. One of Deane's supporters not only threatened but whipped Paine on the streets of Philadelphia.

Two days later, December 17, 1778, a partisan named Matthew Clarkson, who signed himself "Plain Truth," informed the public he would prove "Common Sense" wrong. "Whether this proceeds from ignorance or a worse cause, the Public will hereafter determine."[28] "Plain Truth" jabbed at William Lee by observing in the December 19 issue of the *Pennsylvania Packet:* "Nor shall any person holding any office of profit or trust under the United States, or any of them, accept of any present, emolument, office or title of any kind whatsoever, from any King, Prince or foreign State."

Paine announced on the following day that he would answer "Plain Truth." As Paine rested his proof on dates, resolutions, and letters, "it is impossible to prove him wrong." Paine had no personal concern but "believed the whole affair to be an inflammatory bubble, thrown among the public to answer both a mercantile end and a private pique." He proposed one more article "which will be his last on this bubble of the day."[29]

The *Pennsylvania Packet* of December 21 contained Clarkson's reply to Paine. "Plain Truth" observed that when "Common Sense" announced his intention of entering the lists there had been two schools of thought: (1) Paine would support Deane; (2) by casting a cloud on Deane, Paine would support the friends who had put Paine in office.

The main body of the article recapitulated Deane's affairs. It defended Deane's troubles and accomplishments; it even explained the sending of

French officers in such a way as to reflect credit on Deane and the officers. It printed the official recall and Lovell's accompanying letter to show Deane had no reason to believe it a censure and a disgrace—in fact, the opposite. A postscript announced: "Thomas Paine, like some zealots in religion, wished himself considered as persecuted for the sake of truth."[30]

Deane, on December 21, informed Congress he had committed his report to writing, and requested an early date for the reading. Congress set six o'clock in the evening, December 22. When at that time he did not finish his report, Deane was asked to appear at ten o'clock the following morning. While he was reading next day, he was ordered to withdraw. After prolonged debate and divisions, Deane was ordered to attend on December 28, but a quorum was not then present and he could not continue the report.

The newspaper war continued. The discussion of issues dissolved into name-calling and charges. Paine, on December 28, demanded the name of "Plain Truth." If he did not hear it, he would "order an Attorney to prosecute him as a party concerned in publishing a false malicious libel, tending to injure the reputation of the 'Secretary for Foreign Affairs.' "[31] "Plain Truth" replied: "I laugh at the insolence of office, and despise the threat."[32]

Deane again appeared before Congress on December 31. His request to "communicate personally" parts of his narrative was refused. Congress decided to read "Silas Deane's Narrative," another recapitulation of both missions, with one addition—an account of Arthur Lee's visit to Paris in 1776:

I was in the midst of my affairs with Monsieur Beaumarchais, and was with him every day. My first interview with Mr. Arthur Lee was at the gentleman's house. I afterwards frequently met them together. Mr. Arthur Lee was every day at my lodgings, and I spent all the vacant time I had with him. I acquainted him with my prospects of procuring supplies, and from whom; and he gave me the highest possible character of Mr. Beaumarchais for his abilities and address.[33]

The new year began with the repetition of the old charges and countercharges. Richard Henry Lee blasted Deane in the columns of the *Virginia Gazette* on January 1, 1779, for reflecting upon the good name of his family, but said he had a good conscience.[34] Deane began the year by protesting to

Congress that one Paine, "styling himself Secretary for Foreign Affairs" and pretending to address the public in his official capacity, had ventured to assure the public that supplies which Deane had contracted for with Beaumarchais were a gift of the French government. Paine claimed Arthur Lee had arranged all negotiations before Deane arrived in France and that Paine had in his possession full proof of this fact.[35]

A new factor entered the dispute. Conrad Alexandre Gérard, the French Minister Plenipotentiary to the United States, had watched the battle of words with apprehension. He was too well-trained a diplomat to permit his views to interfere with business. When Paine quoted Arthur Lee's reports from the files of the Committee of Secret Correspondence to prove Deane not responsible for aid from France and that France had intended the assistance as a gift, Gérard could not let it pass unchallenged. He knew his government had supplied the arms and ammunition shipped to the Americans; he also knew France could not admit she had supplied materials to the rebels before recognizing them. The whole operation of secret aid had been to conceal this fact. Paine's position, although unimportant as clerk of the Committee for Foreign Affairs and not Secretary of State, was official, and the only way to combat this claim was that Congress should deny its truth. Gérard demanded this, noting the impropriety of allowing a secretary under oath to divulge anything, much less to publish documents from secret committee files. Upon his insistence Congress after discussion and debate acquiesced, and categorically denied having received help from the French government before the alliance, and relieved Paine from employment. Paine resigned before Congress could discharge him.

"Common Sense" wrote on December 31, that "every state [should] enquire what mercantile connections any of the late or present delegates have had or now have, with Mr. Deane, and that a precedent might not be wanting, it is important that the state of Pennsylvania should begin." Robert Morris replied on January 9, 1779, to what he considered a direct charge by Paine:

> I do not conceive that the state I live in has any right or inclination to enquire into what mercantile connections I have had or now have with Mr. Deane, or with any other person: if Mr. Deane had any commerce that was inconsis-

tent with his public station, he must answer for it; as I did not, by becoming a Delegate from the State of Pennsylvania, relinquish my right of forming mercantile connections, I was at liberty to form such with Mr. Deane. My now giving the account this author desired, is not to gratify him or to resign the right I contend for but purely to remove the force of his insinuation on that subject; and to this effectually, I will candidly relate all the commercial concerns I have had with Mr. Deane.[36]

Three days later Paine attacked those persons engaged in private business while in public life. In his opinion neither Morris nor Deane was capable of judging each other when partners in the same business. He suspected "Plain Truth" and all of Deane's supporters had commercial connections. The column ended with the usual laudatory remarks to the Lees, which again reduced his protest to the partisan level.[37]

Deane inserted the following notice in the *Pennsylvania Packet* for January 14, 1779: "Nothing that Mr. Paine has published could have induced me to alter my resolution to remain silent, until the determination of Congress should be known, and had he not in his wanton madness for abuse, invective and misrepresentation, ventured to state the affairs of the supplies, which were returned by me in France, in a manner totally contrary to the truth, and highly injurious to these States, as well as to justice, honour, and dignity of the Court of France. He has asserted and labored to prove, that those supplies were not a commercial concern, but a present, and that this present was made previous to my arrival in France." He had broken silence because the charges were false. Congress had proof, and the public would learn at the proper time.[38]

The war of words continued to almost ridiculous length. "Philathes" in a tedious article listed twenty falsehoods in all of "Common Sense's" writings.[39] Deane replied to Richard Henry Lee's comment of January 1. Noting that Lee had written, "had I winked at all the information of public abuse I do not think I would have incurred Mr. Deane's censure," Deane asked, "Have I been charged with the abuse of the public trust reposed in me, or with having misapplied public monies?"[40]

Congress refused to charge Deane or release him. In March 1779 Deane reminded the president of Congress of the date of his last unanswered letter. He said his situation for eight months past had been peculiarly distressing and again entreated Congress to inform him if they expected information respecting their foreign or other affairs.[41]

Deane added a postscript in a later letter: "The settlement of the commissioner's accounts and my own will show that I received nothing therefore except money for my necessary expenses." He explained the reason for ignoring attacks in the public print: "From the moment that I was ordered by Congress to lay before them, in writing, a narration of my public transactions I have considered myself as being before that tribunal and not at liberty to take notice of any publication."[42]

In April 1779, for the first time, Deane mentioned his financial interests: "My own family and private affairs, as well as those of one intrusted to my care, have long suffered by my absence; they must suffer to the last degree, if longer delayed."

During the spring and summer of 1779 Deane sent letter after letter to Congress, explaining his position, refuting charges, requesting a hearing.[43] If anything, the newspaper war of words increased in vituperativeness. "Candour," "Lusitania," "Philathes," and other pundits applauded and justified with pens fresh dipped in vitriol. Two charges against Deane were conspicuous: he was "in trade"; and his accounts were in a state of "studied confusion" (to use the language of Arthur Lee).

Congress was not immune from rebuke. The press stated its views in unmistakable terms. An anonymous writer under the caption of "Affairs in Congress," carried in the *Baltimore Advertiser,* June 24, 1779, and reprinted later in the *Virginia Gazette,* and in the *New York Packet,* described the situation as alarming. He took concern from the fact that an organized minority, which he referred to as the Junto, ruled Congress. He traced the Junto back to the first Congress. Originally, he wrote, the Junto was composed of delegates from the North and South against those from New York and one or two middle states. At first members acted together, but recently a club had formed to discuss tactics and strategy. The unknown writer pointed out that as the membership of Congress was constantly changing it was easy for an organized minority to control Congress. The article made clear that unless something was done immediately Congress would continue under the Junto's control.

Congress's action, or inaction, was hardly creditable. It was unable to rise above partisanship. An outstanding example of pettiness, which Henry Laurens described as "droll" in his private notes, occurred on June 10, 1779, when Thomas Burke introduced a resolution seconded by Laurens: "That Silas Deane, Esquire, be ordered not to depart the United States without the special permission of Congress; and that Arthur Lee, Esquire, be directed to repair forwith to America, in order to better enable Congress to enquire into the truth of the several allegations and suggestions made by the said Arthur Lee, in his correspondence with Congress against the said Silas Deane."[44] The motion originated with Laurens who wished to prevent Deane from leaving the country. If Deane did leave without congressional permission, he would be "pleading guilty" to insinuations against him.[45]

Finally, on August 6, 1779, Congress adopted a resolution long advocated by Silas Deane:

> Resolved, that the several Commissioners, Commercial agents, and others in Europe, entrusted with public money, be directed to transmit, without delay, their accounts and vouchers, and also triplicate copies of the same to the Board of Treasury of these United States in order for settlement.

> Resolved, That a suitable person be appointed by Congress to examine the said accounts in Europe, and certify his opinion thereon previous to their being transmitted.

> Resolved, That the Board of Treasury be directed to report for Mr. Deane a reasonable allowance for his time and expenses from the expiration of three months after the notice of his recall to the present time.[46]

Samuel Harrington moved and John Fell seconded the following motion: "Honorable Silas Deane, Esquire, late one of the Commissioners at the Court of Versailles, and political and commercial agent be excused from any further attendance on Congress, in order that he may settle his accounts without delay, agreeable to the foregoing resolution."

The motion was amended to read "discharged" instead of "excused."[47] The reason for the change, as Henry Laurens pointed out to Richard Henry Lee, was "in as much as no provision is made for his voyage to France nor his expenses there, the motion leaves the adjustment of his accounts option with him."[48]

In this terse if not cynical way Congress dismissed Silas Deane with neither censure nor approbation.

CHAPTER 8

DEANE'S

SECOND MISSION TO FRANCE

A new phase of Silas Deane's revolutionary career began with the congressional resolution of August 6, 1779, which, after thirteen months, discharged him from further attendance. The resolution placed the responsibility for settling the accounts squarely upon Deane, at his own time and expense. Deane could have refused this obligation, but to have done so would have forfeited his claims against the government of the United States, as well as supported the accusations of his enemies. He was, of course, determined to clear his name—and secure the money to which he was entitled.

One of the last things Deane did before leaving Philadelphia was to send a memorial to Congress, reminding them that a congressional committee had given him his commission to go abroad and that Congress had ordered him home. Since there then were no charges, he had assumed that Congress approved his conduct as its agent and commissioner. He requested an auditor to examine his accounts in Europe before transmission to America for settlement by the Treasury Board.[1] Such a procedure would prevent error and save time. Because of his neglect of private affairs and the depreciation of the currency, waiting for the settlement of his accounts would mean, he believed, total ruin. He prayed that the examiner make an advance payment subject to audit by the Treasury Board. Congress ignored the memorial but on August 25, 1779, authorized the Treasury Board to issue a warrant to Deane for "ten thousand, five hundred dollars in full consideration for his time and expense during his attendance on Congress from the 4th of June, 1778, until the 6th day of August, inst."[2] The warrant was issued in spite of Laurens's efforts to prevent approval.[3]

Deane wrote his last letter to Congress on November 23, 1779, before going back to France, in which he returned the warrant and explained that in spite of his depleted private fortune he preferred to return to France and vindicate his conduct at his own expense. His refusal to accept the sum did not indicate to Congress the slightest resentment toward men who opposed the grant of even that sum. When he received no answer to his memorial of August 16, he concluded that none would be given.[4]

Before leaving, Deane went to Williamsburg, Virginia, to see his brother Simeon. He had already determined his future conduct: he would avoid political subjects, recoup his fortune, and vindicate himself by settling accounts to the satisfaction of everyone concerned.[5]

From Williamsburg he attempted to rearrange his personal affairs. To his brother Barnabas he committed his only son Jesse, should anything happen.

> I feel much for him, my only hope, and almost the sole object I live for; my other family connections are dear to me, but they are (thank God) capable of providing for themselves, and are in a good way. If any accident happens to me, my son must be yours, and our brother Simeon Deane. I need not remind you of past occurrences in our lives, to urge you to the most attentive and parental care of him; it would argue a doubt of your gratitude and fraternal affection. You will think I write with a gloomy, desponding turn in mind. I do not, but I am not gay.

He gave Barnabas instructions regarding his papers. "You will find among my papers, inventories of all the estate of Mr. Webb, and accounts made out by Joyce [an attorney] under my direction, ready to settle. You will also find an inventory of the notes, &c., payable to me; pray obtain and preserve them." He requested that a "table" be erected to the memory of his second wife "in the same fashion as the first," and that the family select the inscription as she "was equally dear to them as to me." His son Jesse who had accompanied John Adams to France was to remain in Europe for four years to complete his education, and then be placed "to that business which may best suit his inclination and improvement."[6]

One other family matter required attention—painful and unpleasant as it was. To his stepson Joseph Webb he wrote a long letter about personal and legal matters. The tone was affectionate, in no way angry or resentful. He reproached Joseph for silence and urged him not to be a tool in the hands of enemies. He asked sympathy and understanding, not pity.

Turning to the unsettled Webb estate, the source of his stepchildren's resentment, Deane reviewed the impoverished estate at the time he married Joseph's mother, Mehitabel Webb. According to Deane's evaluation, the estate in Wethersfield was now worth about fifteen hundred pounds and represented more than ten of the prime years of his life. Those years had gone, he wrote, "principally in taking care of your interests and education of your brethern. . . . [and] I do not repent of the line of conduct I took up. On the contrary, I reflect on it with pleasure; and the many opportunities afforded me in . . . reflection infinitely greater satisfaction than any which can result from the possession of wealth." But if Joseph insisted on a property settlement, he urged that they try to remove this only possible reason for interruption of the harmony between them since Joseph's infancy. He recommended a disinterested third party to assist in the settlement, in the manner of two friends, "one of whom cannot possibly attend to it himself." "You have an inventory," he wrote, "which will shew you the amount of sums received and paid out; you were privy to the keeping of this account; you have the account made out from the inventory the winter before my leaving Wethersfield. . . . The landed estate left by your honored father has long been divided, and in your possession; you know that it never yielded me any profit at any time; the landed securities are in the same predicament. . . ."

He asked Joseph to explain everything to all members of the family. "I write freely to you, and your brethern ought not to be ignorant of them, for it will affect me sensibly to be thought, and perhaps represented, by them as a defaulter, when I have done not simply legal justice toward them, but have treated them with parental kindness."[7]

Joseph, John, and John Simpson, the husband of Sarah Webb, nonetheless persisted in believing that Silas Deane had sought to defraud them of their inheritance.

[89]

Because of the severity of the winter, the convoy by which Deane planned to return to France was unable to sail until June 20, 1780. He spent the winter attempting to help his brother Simeon, also in financial straits, and gathering the ends of his own affairs. While in Virginia he received letters from friends. From Robert Morris he obtained, in addition to a business offer, words that must have pleased him: "Reflecting on unrestricted abuse you have suffered, and not knowing whether you have any evidence with you to shew that your particular friends were not infected with the pestilence of the times, I have suddenly and hastily scribbled a letter to Doctor Franklin . . ."[8]

True to his word, Morris wrote Franklin: "I consider Mr. Deane as a martyr in the cause of America. After rendering the most signal and important Services, he has been reviled and traduced in the most shameful manner. But I have not a doubt the day will come when his merit shall be universally acknowledged, and the authors of those calumnies held in the detestation they deserve."[9]

Deane embarked on his return voyage, the monotony of the forty-two-day sea trip broken by capture of two prizes and loss of a merchant ship in convoy. The convoy slipped by a British blockading squadron and arrived in Bordeaux on July 25, 1780. Deane was later to learn they were fortunate as "few vessells escaped" the blockading fleet.[10]

Upon arrival he notified Franklin he was in France and proceeding to Paris. After a few days he went to Passy, where he was cordially received. "I have taken my old lodging with Dr. Franklin," he wrote, "and do not find my character to have suffered here by the abuse I met with in America during my absence from France." He received a kind and hearty welcome from Chaumont, Beaumarchais, and other friends. Deane appreciated his reception, which helped him forget faction and cabal elsewhere. From Spain, John Jay sent a belated but sincere letter expressing faith and confidence.

Although Deane was grateful for kind words and tokens of esteem, he realized his precarious financial condition would not permit delay. He had several schemes to recoup his fortune. The immediate object was settling his accounts, but he was also planning for the future. He intended to re-enter mercantile business and take up speculation in western lands.

As a former merchant he anticipated few difficulties in the mercantile business. Because of the demand for goods created by the war and lack of trade with England, he did not expect difficulty establishing himself. He was known in French mercantile circles and had a private account with Grand, the banker for the American commission in Paris, with whom he planned to finance his venture.[11] Unfortunately, perhaps because they planned to go into business together, he had given Chaumont power to draw upon his funds.[12] To his surprise he soon found his bills protested.[13] He had brought with him loan-office certificates which he had expected to sell in France for a commission. He wrote his friend Isaac Moses that he had not sent a shilling on any account, owing to unexpected disappointment.[14] Because of inflation and the attempted deflation of the American currency at a forty-to-one ratio, French interest in American trade and investment was nil. Without capital or credit, Deane's prospects faded.

The greatest blow came when he failed to obtain a contract to supply American masts for the French and Spanish navies. John Jay, pressing the contract at the Spanish court, was not hopeful. He wrote Deane, "The more I enquire and hear about your contract the more I am convinced it will never be ratified."[15] Finally, Deane was forced to admit that the Spanish ministers were "disposed to know nothing of us either in public or private." To James Wilson, his associate in America, he reported uncertainty about the French contract. His contract specified no payment until the masts had been delivered to French ports and approved by officials of the Marine Ministry. Without convoys, delivery was impossible. "Thus, to all appearances, this is like to be suspended during the war. The embarrassment in which I have found a certain gentleman of whom I had depended here, has hurt me in this affair, as well as in some others, exceedingly. In short, I despair of doing anything in this affair, or in the land way, so long as the war continues . . ."[16]

Likewise he failed to make headway with western lands. Like many other Americans of his day, Deane early had acquired interest in such lands.[17] He had planned to engage in some large-scale land speculations, until the need arose to return to France to settle his accounts.[18] While in Williamsburg waiting for the convoy to sail, he received a proposition which would permit him to carry out his idea on perhaps an even larger scale. Robert Morris had suggested that he investigate selling undeveloped American lands in France.[19] The operation included Joseph Wharton and James Wilson.

Deane would be advance agent in Europe with one-fourth interest in lands purchased. Wharton would handle the business in Philadelphia, obtaining grants and descriptions. Deane would sell a third, half, or more, as he thought best.[20]

Deane wrote James Wilson soon after arrival that although he had not had time to discuss land speculations, he thought the prospects good.[21]Gérard, now former French minister to the United States, was a likely representative to interest French speculators.[22] To John Shee, who was not a member of the Philadelphia group, Deane wrote he felt he could do something with his shares of the Illinois and Wabash lands "but I fear your limits are higher than they will go at." He promised to keep Shee's lands in mind and keep in touch.[23]

Deane continued to interest French speculators, but the desire to sell was stronger in America than the desire to buy in France. In June 1781 Robert Morris asked for information concerning sales. Robert R. Livingston, the future Secretary of the Committee for Foreign Affairs, was said to consider sale of some lands.[24] Nothing happened. By September, Deane expressed discouragement to James Wilson: "No one will have anything to do at present with land adventures in America, and very few with any other. Its being known that a merchant has made, or is about to make, any considerable adventure in America, is of itself sufficient to hurt his credit in France at this time."[25]

One by one Deane's hopes faded. He had left America confident of clearing his name and regaining financial standing. One disappointment followed another. To Barnabas he wrote: "My patience is exhausted, and my affairs ruined by the unexampled conduct of Congress, who have detained me here—it is now more than a year—waiting for the appointment of an auditor to settle my accounts, which in reality I believe they never wish to have settled."[26] He wrote sadly to James Wilson:

For myself, almost everything I depended upon when I left America has failed. I built great hopes on the mast contract, and had good right so to do at the time. I presume that something might be done with lands, and I flattered myself that our public credit was not so low in Europe, but that Loan Office Certificates would sell for at least what they cost in America; but in particular I was confident that Congress, after suffering me to be calumniated as a public defaulter, and in effect treating me as such themselves, would certainly have an auditor ready to meet me in the examination and settlement of my accounts, and that they would seek rather than avoid a scrutiny; but I have not been less deceived in this than in my other expectations.[27]

Some disappointments resulted from the unsettled economic and political conditions, but the greatest blow in these difficult times was the failure of Congress to settle his accounts. Not only was he ruined financially; the tactics and methods used to circumvent the settlement with Congress broke his spirit. Congress had intended to settle with Deane after his accounts were audited. By indiscreet words and letters Deane enabled his enemies to blacken his name with charges, and it was impossible for friends to defend either his conduct or to press for settlement of his claims.

The settlement of the commissioners' accounts, for which Deane had primarily returned to France in July 1780, had different values for the men involved. To Deane it meant financial independence. To Franklin it meant the end of a distasteful and involved piece of business. Franklin was to learn that it had been whispered he had opposed settling Deane's accounts. He resented the charge and correctly attributed it to Arthur Lee and Ralph Izard.[28] He praised Deane's great service to the Revolution and thought him entitled to a fair hearing and compensation. When Franklin learned of the decision of Congress to have the accounts of all commissioners audited, he expressed approval to James Lovell. Franklin likewise volunteered his opinion of Deane: "I had, and still have, a very good opinion of Mr. Deane for his zeal and activity in the service of his country . . . and as yet I think him innocent."[29] Lovell, an ardent champion of the Lees, naturally disagreed.

The intention of Congress appeared clearly when Joshua Johnson of Nantes was appointed to audit the commissioners' accounts. At first Johnson refused to accept the assignment, but consented when Franklin showed him a congressional order. By agreement he postponed the examination of Deane's account until Deane arrived from America.[30] Franklin was anxious to finish the auditing and appreciated Johnson's willingness to undertake it. Shortly before Deane's arrival Franklin wrote Johnson: "I grow more impatient to have those accounts settled; if, therefore, Mr. Deane should not arrive in the course of a month I must then desire you would come up. Bring with you, if you can, a good clerk that is an accountant, to copy, etc., and let us do the business together as well as we can."[31] Unfortunately, when Johnson reversed his decision, Deane was in America waiting for the weather to permit sailing.

When Deane landed in France he began closing his accounts, but what he expected to be an affair of a few months became tedious and perplexing. He wrote Robert Morris in September 1780: "I am now engaging on a full settlement, or, rather, to state in a clear and simple point of view every transaction I have been concerned in, in Europe, and flatter myself that I shall get through in a few weeks, in a manner that will justify your good opinion of me; and the results I am confident will not cause you or any others to blush for having been my friend."[32] The same month he wrote John Jay commenting on his progress and contrasting Congress's treatment of the other commissioners.

> I greatly wish to see you, but the settling the Commissioners account must take up some time here. You know that the only objections against me in America were on the score of those accounts having been left unsettled; yet Mr. Adams returned to America without settling even his private accounts, th' he had not any other business, nor did anything else in Europe but spend money and keep the accounts. No fault was found with him, but he was honorably reappointed. Mr. [Arthur] Lee, who remained in France, more than a year after his recall, has not settled either his public or private accounts. Mr. Izard, Mr. William Lee are in the same predicament. These men have, each of them, as appears by these accounts, received more than twice the amount of public monies which I ever received, and have literally done worse than nothing.[33]

Deane's correspondence during the autumn of 1780 consisted primarily of letters to merchants and to Joshua Johnson asking explanations of items charged him instead of the commissioners jointly. When Deane informed Johnson that he had nearly closed other accounts, he had yet to learn of Johnson's refusal to audit his accounts.[34]

As 1780 drew to a close, Deane wrote John Paul Jones who was also having troubles with Arthur Lee: "Meantime I can only say that no man feels more sensibly than I do for the disappointments you have met with; every one who knows anything of my history will believe what I say, but I have never lost sight of the great object, or suffered my ardor to abate on account of anything I have met with, and I am confident that you are and will be animated with the same principle."[35] At the time Deane was living on money borrowed from Vergennes. In December 1780 he expressed belief that he could soon repay the loan as his "accounts were almost finally and fully stated."[36]

The beginning of 1781 was not auspicious, for Deane learned that Johnson had refused to audit his accounts and Franklin had no authorization to advance funds. On February 3, 1781, he summed up his position to Jay:

> I have nearly closed all my accounts, public as well as private, but Mr. Johnson, the auditor appointed by Congress, refused to act, and Doctor Franklin says he cannot act, nor can he even pay any part of the considerable sum due to me without orders from Congress. Thus, my Dear Sir, I have been abused in America as a defaulter, whilst a large sum was due me, obliged to return to Europe at my own expense to settle the public accounts, and now am refused payment under pretense that the accounts and vouchers must first be examined and passed by Congress. I do not blame Doctor Franklin; he is sensible to my situation, and acts the friendly part, but his hands are tied by Congress.[37]

To friends and brothers in America he repeated the story. He wrote Simeon: "I have thought of venturing once more to America with my accounts, but the uncertainty in which I am with respect to everything there deters me from resolving decisively."[38]

Several months later he wrote James Wilson that his accounts had been ready for six months and Congress had known for over a year that Johnson would not audit them.[39] But Congress, so far as he knew, had failed to designate another auditor. His financial situation was desperate. He now dwelled constantly on his inability to collect a single sou for support and the failure of Congress to appoint an auditor. Deane settled the public accounts of his fellow commissioners as well as his own. For his services Congress owed him three hundred thousand livres—a sum based on the time Deane had served as agent for the Secret Committee of Correspondence. By his contract with the committee he was to receive a five percent commission on goods sent to America. For services as commissioner, Deane charged only his living expenses.[40]

Again Deane appealed to Congress. He told the old story of Johnson's refusal to accept appointment and Congress's failure to designate another auditor. He admitted his condition: "My necessities would have long since have justified my seizing on the public property here to the amount of the money due me; but I have withheld from doing it on the account of my regard for the credit of my country, and have rather chosen to be obliged to strangers for money for my support." To the charge that he had grown rich on public money he showed how his situation and accounts gave the lie. All he requested was simple justice.[41]

Month by month he lived in hope of justice, faith that Congress would act honorably. When he learned of the acceptance of Arthur Lee's accounts, he reconsidered and sent his own accounts to Philadelphia.[42] Hope revived in September 1781, when he learned that Congress had ordered a vice consul, Robert Barclay, to settle accounts in Europe. In fact, Congress ordered a copy of the resolution sent to Deane.[43]

Early in the autumn Deane moved to Ghent because he could live there more cheaply. When he received the resolution from Congress announcing Robert Barclay's appointment, he eagerly arranged a meeting which produced an unexpected surprise: the vice consul's instructions did not cover Deane's accounts.[44] At first Deane refused to believe Barclay and did so only after he had seen a copy of his instructions.[45] Both he and Barclay agreed that Congress had intended differently by the resolution of September 12, 1781, a copy of which went to Deane. Someone, they, concluded, was playing a grim joke.

The story Barclay told Deane bore the signs of chicanery. As Deane related the story to Barnabas, what happened became more clear:

> He [Barclay] even told me that, supposing a settlement with me would be one part of his instructions, he had applied for particular directions on the subject, and had received for answer that Congress did not mean that he should have anything to do in that affair. Enclosed you have the resolution of Congress, and I leave you to judge whether after such manoeuvres (I am not disposed to give them the name they merit) I can expect justice from the people at large, deceived and irritated by men capable of going such lengths.[46]

The whole affair was a great blow to Deane's morale. In desperation he requested Barclay to write Congress for new instructions. He sought money from the vice consul by citing as precedent the Act of Congress granting

Beaumarchais an advance pending settlement of his accounts.[47] Barclay agreed to the first request, but declined the second, since he was not authorized to expend money without a congressional order. Barclay, who sympathized with Deane, agreed to audit the accounts unofficially to prevent delay should any change of orders come from Congress.[48] Deane also wrote his brothers asking their influence with members of Congress.

The final blow came in 1782 when Barclay informed Deane that the Secretary of the Committee of Foreign Affairs would inform him of the decision. Deane received this information after he went to London.

CHAPTER 9

ACCUSATIONS OF BETRAYAL

DURING the last period of Deane's work in Europe, especially toward the last part of his second mission to France, the argument appeared that he had "sold out" the cause of the Revolution—that he had failed to champion his country's friends against its enemies, had made enormous profits in Europe, and generally acted in such a way that it might be assumed he could have come into the pay of Great Britain. What was the truth of this charge? Did such arguments contain even some elements of truth?

Perhaps some of the difficulty lay in Deane's habit of talking and writing to excess. Almost immediately after returning to France, he had criticized certain Americans there and the conduct of the war in America. These sentiments he had expressed freely and openly. In America he had long been considered anti-American and anti-French, particularly after the publication of some of his private letters in the Tory press of New York. These letters, long political essays on the nature of government and the origin of the quarrel with Great Britain, gave joy to his enemies and forced his friends to abandon him or remain quiet. Deane regretted the outbreak of hostilities, questioned the sincerity of the French alliance, and urged careful consideration of the British terms of reconciliation.[1]

The letters deserve some explanation. During his first mission in France, Deane had considered it a duty, as indeed it was, to report to the Secret Committee of Correspondence his observations on political and economic conditions in France and Europe. He had corresponded freely with the

Congressional agent in Holland, Dumas. Upon returning to France, he resumed the practice of writing to his friends, this time with disastrous results. Deane was basically an honest man. His letters contained his evaluation of the times, and were for the information of his friends. In a sense, his honesty was the root of his troubles. In France he discovered Americans who felt it their duty to speak only of the good points of the American scene and to ignore, deny, or distort undesirable features or conditions. Deane could not tolerate this false sense of patriotism.

The charge that he had enriched himself—that he had made sixty thousand pounds by speculation and private trade during his duties in France—is not justified by the facts. Before he returned to Paris, he had admitted financial embarrassment to Congress in his memorial of August 18, 1779. He estimated the cost of the return from France in 1778, and his fourteen months waiting in Philadelphia at fifty thousand dollars.[2]

Deane naturally grew critical of his country. He was greatly disturbed by the change in French public opinion regarding America and Americans. "The enthusiasm with which France embraced our cause and us at first, is gone," he wrote William Duer, "and the resolution of Congress of 18th of March last, irretrevably [sic] damned our credit and honor. Add to this the success of England at sea, and the language held by Lee and others, and especially by Adams, who not only in private, but in letters to the minister, has asserted that America is not obliged to France, but on the contrary, that England will settle with us at any price."[3] Deane also "attentively" examined and reviewed the state of American affairs in Europe. He believed these affairs had never been in a more critical state than at that moment, and that nothing but a speedy peace would prevent the most ruinous consequence. These melancholy observations were made to his old neighbor in Connecticut, Thomas Mumford, who, he felt, would not "misuse" confidence by making any part of it public.[4]

Deane did not limit his correspondence to friends in America. To John Jay in Spain he had made some exceedingly derogatory comments. He deplored the loss of American credit and prestige in Europe: "it is almost as great a disgrace to be known to be American as it was two years since an honor." He complained of the number of representatives, "almost thirteen," sent by Congress and the individual states, "who are foolishly making a parade and bidding on each other."[5]

He distrusted France and criticized her for "spinning out the war" instead of making a decisive stroke. France had underestimated the time required to defeat Great Britain; in the meantime America would be ruined.[6] To the same correspondent he later wrote: "My best wishes are for Peace, Safety and Liberty of America. . . . But the situation of America wrings my very soul." He feared the twenty thousand French troops in America would cause the loss of the struggle for independence. "The only actual object is, if England or France and Spain shall in the future give the law." He felt it a "dreadful alternative to be reduced to the choice of tyrants after having risqued everything to conquer one."[7]

It is unfortunate that Deane did not limit his frank observations to friends or use more discretion in putting remarks on paper. Even his French friends lost heart. By December 1780 his remarks led Beaumarchais to make certain pointed suggestions to Vergennes. Beaumarchais was unaware that Vergennes was already privately lending money to Deane. According to Beaumarchais, "he was the only person in whom he [Deane] has entirely confided, and he shows a bitterness that borders on something worse. I am myself so embarrassed that I can offer him only temporary assistance. . . . Mr. Deane is a partizan of France, and his devotion accounts for nearly all his enemies in America." Beaumarchais admitted that Deane was uneasy, observing his profound emotion in talking of his country, himself, his son in school in Paris, his present situation, and the ingratitude that had occasioned it. Beaumarchais's remedy was for France to advance a sum for Deane's support rather than permit defection—"a grave political error."[8]

Soon the Lees were in full cry against Deane. In December 1780 William Lee informed Arthur Lee: "Your former minister, Mr. Silas Deane, we are told, since his return to France, has been continually employed in invectives against his country. According to him, America is ruined, and must be subjected by England; therefore all the aid France gives is so much thrown away. We are surprised at this, as he lives at Passy with your minister, and seems to be his favorite and prime councillor. Mr. Deane adds, also, that your grand Congress is composed of fools and knaves; we hope he has not experienced them to be so."[9]

Deane became a virtual defeatist. Francis Dana, an American visiting in Paris, reported Deane's critical attitude toward Congress and fear of the military situation. Dana based his remarks on a long conversation with

Deane. Deane said America was already conquered; the power of Great Britain was steadily rising while that of her enemies was almost spent; Holland would be defeated and the armed neutrality crushed; in self-interest Europe should support England rather than America; Congress, a cipher, had lost influence everywhere in America. Finally, he apologized for Arnold's desertion. Dana reported keeping his temper while he heard Deane out.[10]

Many individuals in both Europe and America were not ready to hear Deane out. In Spain, John Jay learned from William Carmichael, Deane's former associate in France and now in Spain as Jay's secretary, of statements attributed to Deane. Jay sent a sharp warning: "You must be sensible that such reports will be no less prejudicial to you in America than in Europe."[11] Deane replied he could easily guess, but did not name, the source of Carmichael's information. Deane said he expected to be called a Tory and an enemy of America. He had often been called to justify acts of Congress, especially the Act of March 18, 1780, which reduced the value of currency to a forty-to-one ratio. He avoided going into company as far as he decently could. He expressed bitterness against Americans who misrepresented conditions in America. He related in detail the story of a Mr. Searle, a member of Congress, who arrived in Paris a few weeks after he did. According to Searle, Washington's army consisted of twenty thousand men; recruits were pressing to enlist; America did not wish peace until "that old lion's claws should be cut and his teeth drawn." The United States could carry on the war alone. Commerce injured America, and American merchants were rogues and speculators; French merchants who complained of the depreciation were speculators and peddlers. Goods from France had done more harm than forty thousand Russians sent to fight against the states. If his assertions were doubted, so Deane told Jay, Searle answered contemptuously: "You will pardon me, good Sir, I am a member of Congress, the only man that ever came over to Europe in that character. I must know, I have been chairman of most of their committees. I think I ought to know." Deane reported many such Americans in Paris who went almost as far as Searle in distorting conditions in America.

In spite of warnings from friends and his own resolutions to avoid political discussions, Deane could not refrain from controversy. He corrected the remarks of other Americans. He wrote John Jay that he did not consider it honorable or wise to remain silent after he had warned French ministers that the chaotic state of the American forces, finances, and commerce required supplies or money and fleet immediately. "I did," he stated, "what I trust you and every other honest American would have done, I told the truth."

Deane knew Dana and Searle had reported him to America as an enemy. He maintained, however, his concern for the welfare of America. Deane questioned Jay: "Was it inimical for me to declare the same thing five months since, and to do everything which a private individual could do to persuade the minister of the real wants and dangerous situation of America?"[12] Jay approved Deane's honest statement to the ministers of France, but questioned how far it was necessary or prudent to mention the same thing in private conversations.[13]

It may perhaps be concluded that the stress and strain of revolution places all men in one of three camps. Those who favor revolution are patriots or traitors; those who oppose it are loyalists or traitors. Those who attempt to be dispassionate become objects of contempt and are called traitors by both their patriot and loyalist countrymen. The patriot who supports the cause and then recants becomes an object of hatred. The turncoat's name becomes a synonym for traitor and a curse in the language of the nation: such was the fate of Benedict Arnold. Likewise the revolutionary generation accused and condemned Silas Deane.

His former associates accused Silas Deane of betraying the Revolution for "thirty pieces of silver." Deane did lack funds during the last ten years of his life, but the accusation that he received financial assistance from the British cannot be documented. Doubtless British Intelligence was aware of his plight and attempted to exploit his position. The correspondence between King George III and Lord North reveals that they considered attempting to use Deane. There was nothing so crude as a direct approach. In March 1781 George III wrote Lord North "I think it perfectly right that Mr. Deane should be so far trusted as to have three thousand pounds in goods for America; giving him particular instructions would be liable to much hazard . . ."[14] The first part of the sentence implies that North had considered an approach. The second indicates that George III did not deem it wise to give Deane instructions that might lead him to believe that the offer of financial assistance came from a British agent or the government.

The adventure came to nothing; no further mention occurs in either Deane's papers or the George III-North correspondence.

The first the public in America knew of Deane's rumored defection from the revolutionary cause was the publication of some letters purportedly written in May and June 1781 and taken from an American ship captured by the British navy. After examination, Lord North sent them to the commanding general of the British forces in America, Sir Henry Clinton, with a covering letter saying they were intercepted letters which might have some "utility." North refused to disclose the source of the letters, saying it would be better for the "reader to guess."[15]

In the George III-North correspondence, discussion of the "intercepted letters" is contradictory. The assumption is that the English had bought the letters, but they were too pro-British to be satisfactory. In the same correspondence both the king and the minister mention and even quote other letters. George III wrote North: "I have received Lord North's boxes containing the intercepted letters from Mr. Deane for America. I have only been able to read two of [them], on which I form the same opinion of too much appearance of being concerted with this country, and therefore not likely to have the effect as if they bore another aspect." North also thought them "too strong in our favour to bear the spontaneous opinion, but that, if supposed to authentick, they will see they have by concert fallen into our hands."

These letters seem to prove that Deane was in the pay of the British government. But why should the king pay for and send to America something neither he nor his first minister approved? If Deane had agreed to sell out, why did he not write or permit the foreign office to write letters which would please George III? Yet there is no mention of returning the letters or of asking Deane to rewrite them. Evidence of other intercepted letters appears in the king's letter of July 19 to North: "The extract from Franklin is very material; should France not supply America amply, I think it has the appearance that this contest will end as it ought, by the colonies returning to the mother country; and I confess I will never put my hand to any other conclusion of this business."[16] As British Intelligence was skilled in the acquisition of letters without their owner's permission, securing Deane's and Franklin's letters would be a minor detail in the day's work of any good agent.

Deane learned of the publication of his letters from Robert Barclay, the vice consul whom he thought Congress had appointed to settle his accounts. He wrote his brother, Barnabas, he was not sorry the letters had been published: "Disagreeable as this circumstance must be to me, I shall not be sorry to have all America informed of my sentiments, and the grounds on which they are founded. I have seen nothing since to alter my way of thinking, but on the contrary much to confirm me in it."[17] Not having seen the New York publication, Deane was not certain his letters had been doctored. He admitted he did not "know what Rivington [the printer] may have published, but I well know what I wrote. I have carefully examined the copies of my letters, and I find nothing in them but what every free subject has a right to say or write or publish in the most open manner to the world, without being liable to be censured, much less to be punished therefor." He ridiculed the charge of having been privy to Arnold's treachery, as too ridiculous and absurd to merit attention. "My opinion of his conduct is the same at this time which it has ever been from my first hearing of his defection, and it is, that after those who, by their ingratitude and abuse toward him, pushed him on to those desperate measures, have taken on themselves their full share of the guilt of his treachery, there will still remain enough to render him criminal in the eyes of honest men."[18]

Deane denied selling out to the British. He considered himself a victim of the intolerance of the day, for daring to speak and write honestly and frankly as a private citizen. In a letter to his brother Barnabas he reviewed the charges and defended his right to an opinion. He pointed out that since he held no public trust he could not violate it. He deplored his government's denying a citizen the right to express an opinion to friends. Questioning the wisdom of political democracy for America, the sincerity and disinterestedness of the French, and condemning certain proceedings of Congress—these things did not make him a traitor. He denied the British had bribed him. "I have asserted nothing in my letters which is not most notoriously true." He doubted a "poor persecuted exile" could say anything to hurt the American cause and pointed to his miserable circumstances to prove he had gained nothing for his honesty but abusive insinuations from personal and political enemies.[19]

Deane argued he had as much to gain by success of the Revolution as anyone else in America. His fortune, three hundred thousand livres, was in the hands of Congress. It was not likely he would bring about the "destruction of that body." He asked what inducement a British minister could have to purchase him as he had neither trust nor employment and was too unpopular in America ever to expect any. Intrigues of the party in power had brought about his persecution and exile. His hope rested on pecuniary justice from Congress. "In such a situation, is it possible that any man of common reflection can conceive me to be a subject of importance to the British ministry? If I had had the forces or finances of my country or any important negociation [sic] committed to my direction, the case would have been widely different; but as ministers of state, any more than other men, give money without some object in view, equal at least to the advances made, the question recurs, what object could they have in view in advancing money to me?"

Deane was charged with changing sides for money. But, as he pointed out, "my distressed situation at Paris, and at this moment [January 1782] on account of money for my support, sufficiently proves that if I really sold myself to the British government, I forgot the most essential article in the bargain, and received nothing in exchange. I am at this moment indebted to Doctor Franklin and others at Paris for sums borrowed for my support, and, being unable to pay, am obliged to their kindness even for my personal liberty."[20]

Men who make revolutions have too much at stake to judge wisely those accused of deviating from the revolutionary line. In all honesty, Deane might protest his right to express opinions to his friends, but his countrymen judged his remarks and drew conclusions. Friends remained loyal to him when it was reported that he was making remarks about Congress, the conduct of the war, and the duplicity of France. The publication of his "intercepted letters" raised doubts as to their authenticity among his friends; but when he acknowledged their authenticity, they could no longer champion his cause. Many, no doubt for self-protection, joined the hue against him.

Gradually the ring closed around him. Robert R. Livingston, now Secretary of the Committee for Foreign Affairs, warned Jay against communication with Deane, and urged "you will doubtless use every means in your power to destroy the ill effects which his calumnies may have had upon the minds of people with you." Livingston informed Congress that "measures have long been taken to put our ministers on guard against Mr. Deane."[21] Thomas Paine, Deane's former antagonist, wrote Robert Morris: "I hope that man's knack of creating confusion and involving characters in suspicion is at an end. Whether the letters be genuine or not I do not Undertake to give judgement upon, but his language [in France] is equally strange as anything contained in these publications."[22] James Madison commented to Edmund Pendleton:

> The genuineness of some of these letters is upon good ground questioned, but more of them contain marks of authenticity which clearly denounce him to be an apostate, and consign his character to the same infamy with that of his friend Arnold. This sentence is delivered here against him with the less hesitation because a prior and indubitable evidence of his degeneracy had been received through another channel. Whether this defection had proceeded, from a mercenary contract with the enemy, from a view of obtaining such an one, or from a chagrin at the obstacle which his country has by a total prohibition of intercourse with the enemy opposed to the commercial projects he went to Europe to execute is as yet a matter of speculation.[23]

Later, Madison informed Pendleton "on which ever side Mr. Deane's letters are viewed they present mysteries."[24] Pendleton replied: "I have long given up Deane as an unworthy man whom I thought much otherwise when I served with him in Congress."[25] Oliver Wolcott told a friend that he and others believed Deane's letters genuine.[26] "Mr. Deane has fully proved himself to be a traytor to his country. . . . The ministry of Great Britain certainly f[ound] his price and have given it him," was the opinion of Nicholas Everleigh of New York.[27]

Congress took no notice of the apostasy of its former commissioner. However, James Lovell, the secretary, informed Robert Morris that although Congress thought it beneath their dignity to pass a resolution changing the name of the *Deane,* a United States vessel of war, another name would be more agreeable and a change justified because the person after whom the ship was named had by his perfidy and defection forfeited title to every mark of honor and respect.[28]

Arthur Lee's reaction to the "intercepted letters" was both curious and typical. Lee complained that "the defection of Mr. Deane seems not to have drawn any punishment nor even odium upon his one time friends and associates."[29]

Washington, who had approved Deane's conduct in July 1778, now declared: "I wish never to hear or see anything more of so infamous a character." Washington wrote Governor Trumbull of Connecticut, expressing satisfaction for the letter in which Trumbull had offered not only his personal opinion but also the sentiment of his state's legislative body.[30]

Soon no one trusted Deane. Joseph Reed, a onetime friend, wrote to General Greene that he rejoiced in the detection of Deane's schemes, although it was unfortunate that Deane's "friends, partners, supporters, and abettors, appear in public, unblushing, and join in the cry of infamy as cordially as if they had neither been in the counsel, or participation in the profits of iniquity."[31] Benjamin Tallmadge bluntly informed Deane "that the epithet of Traitor is freely bestowed on you . . ."[32] Elkanah Watson, after an interview with Deane in Ghent, decided "Deane must be regarded an enemy alike to France and America."[33] Robert Livingston confirmed this opinion to John Jay: "No doubt is entertained here of his apostasy, or of his endeavour to weaken the efforts of the United States, and to traduce the character of the people and their rulers, both in Europe and America."[34]

Even Benjamin Franklin conceded a change in Deane. Franklin had praised Deane in 1778 when he had been recalled, and welcomed him at Passy in 1780, when he returned to France. He had heard of, but refused to believe, Deane's repudiation of the Revolution. In March 1782 he admitted to Robert R. Livingston that Deane had changed. He acknowledged the intercepted letters as genuine and said Deane now lived in Ghent, distressed both in mind and circumstances. A recent twenty-page letter from Deane was filled with abuse of Congress, self-justification and vindication of Arnold's conduct. He feared Deane had ruined himself in America and France and would shortly join Arnold in England.[35]

Although many people believed Deane had betrayed the Revolution, his brothers and many friends did not then or ever believe Deane had committed treason. Barnabas feared Silas's letters would ruin him, "although they may contain only the truth" and expressed surprise at his brother's imprudence in writing so freely.[36] Simeon wrote that coffeehouse talk was "needless and improper, but they suspect treason." He resented the treatment

Deane had received from Congress, and closed with a declaration of faith: "I trust, my dear brother, that you are sure that I bear you the most affectionate regard, and would risque my life most freely where it might be of service to your just reputation; but at present what can be done? To oppose a torrent is madness; to sit down quiet, impossible."[37]

This second mission to France thus was a series of bitter defeats. Deane's attempts to regain financial independence by business enterprises came to nothing. He made no progress in settling his accounts with Congress. His enemies called him a profiteer, then changed the charge to one of treason.

Was Deane a traitor? To set out the circumstances of the accusation is at once to bring doubt that he was. Moreover, no one ever proved his defection from the cause of his country. After all, nearly two centuries have passed since the revolutionary era. Some proof, one would think, should have emerged. One is reminded of other historical controversies in which it has long been fashionable to argue the guilt of individuals without proof. It is the task of historians to avoid such assertions until proof appears.

Again, when the circumstances surrounding Silas Deane's second mission to France are examined, it is clear why he came to trouble in the minds of his countrymen. Given the type of man he was, full of suspicion, deeply disappointed by the successful maneuvers of his enemies, it was natural that opinion turned against him, and that his frankness took opinion even to the point of believing him a traitor.

CHAPTER 10

DEANE IN ENGLAND

THE War for American Independence ended with Cornwallis's surrender at Yorktown on November 18, 1781. Provisional articles of peace, signed November 30, 1781, recognized independence. Formal separation of Great Britain and the thirteen colonies occurred with the peace treaty of September 3, 1783. Silas Deane had been wrong about the outcome of the conflict: France had continued to support the Revolution with men and material; Great Britain had lost the war; peace was now a reality.

But for Deane there was no peace. The end of the war found him in a precarious position. For eighteen months he had been living in Ghent in physical distress and mental anguish. To John Jay he had described the conditions of the past eighteen months—barely decent lodging, no servant, meals at the common table. Only rigid economy kept him from extreme want. Even this subsistence depended on the generosity of a friend in Paris. His inability to provide for his son added gall to his cup.[1]

Many persons were aware that Deane was enduring hardships in Ghent, but those who knew him best feared for his sanity. As early as December 1780 Beaumarchais reported to Vergennes his uneasiness upon Deane's profound emotion and "bitterness that borders on something worse."[2] Two years later, Franklin wrote of Deane's distress in mind and circumstances: "He continues . . . to sit croaking at Ghent, chagrined, discontented and dispirited."[3] Deane himself wrote Connecticut Governor Trumbull admitting it was not improbable his private losses and the ingratitude and injustice had affected a mind unfortunately not gay and volatile but serious and gloomy, so that he viewed things through a dark and discolored medium which often magnified shadows and annihilated realities.[4]

When the war was over, Deane felt peace would calm men's minds. Of his own position he wrote:

> an individual will not be regarded as an enemy because, in the hour of his despondency, and apprehensions for his country, he imprudently attempted to warn his countrymen of what he thought their danger; . . . It is true that I wrote many [letters] to my private friends, for their information; it is equally true that some of those letters were basely betrayed, and that others were intercepted and published in New York, not to serve Great Britain so much as to injure me; and for that purpose some of them were altered in many parts, and the whole placed in the most unfavorable light. Though I am ready to acknowledge that I was misinformed and misled in some, and even in many, things, and that I was imprudent to write or speak at all on the subject, yet as a free citizen, I had a right to do both; nor will I ever part with that right of speaking and writing my sentiments on the state and the management of the public affairs of my country; but I shall, from what has past, be more on my guard in the future.[5]

He strongly felt that trade between Great Britain and North America would resume. He had an unsettled account in London which he was sure he could settle if he were there. A letter to John Jay tells of the account and explains that he hoped "for some advantage from being among the first in sending out goods to America." Deane asked Jay for an opinion, as he knew his countrymen would take it ill should he go to London, although hostilities were suspended and everyone at liberty to go there.[6] Jay advised that such a move would be imprudent, since Americans already suspected Deane of working for the British.[7]

Although he urgently needed to go to London, Deane did not leave Ghent until the commissioners in Paris had "no objections."[8] Arriving in London late in March 1783, he took a room at 135 Fleet Street.

His appearance immediately started rumors confirming what his enemies claimed was true. His friends could not deny them. His interest continued to be the settlement of his accounts, and he retained contact with Barclay in hope the vice consul would receive instructions which would make settlement feasible. In April 1783 Barclay informed Deane that Congress had sent instructions and that he would show them.[9] The instructions proved a new disappointment. Barclay was ordered to refer any questionable item to Congress for settlement, and not authorized to advance funds.[10] Congress reserved the right to approve the time and manner of the final settlement.

Deane confided to Beaumarchais in April 1784 that Congress had no intention of settling the accounts. "Mr. Barclay," he explained, "has been with me to examine my accounts. But his instructions from Congress are such that it is impossible to settle with him. I can tell you freely that I think them drawn up in that manner with design." He revealed the old bitterness when he wrote:

> Men who have no disposition to pay are often ingenious at putting off a settlement. He, Mr. Barclay, has orders to pass no articles of account without the most explicit vouchers; to pay no regard to any settlement already made without examining of it himself; and for merchandize and stores shipped to America, he is ordered to enquire if they were of good quality, if they were charged at a just price, by whom they were shipped, &c., &c. . . . Yes, Sir, the quality, price, and quantity of those very arms and stores which enabled their army in 1777 to triumph over General Burgoyne, and decided the fate of the United States, are now minutely enquired into, and you are to receive no more money until the result of the enquiry shall be approved by Congress.[11]

In June 1784 Barclay transmitted to Robert Morris, the Superintendent of Finance, a copy of Deane's accounts "as settled by himself," to which Barclay added remarks, none of which seemed of consequence.[12] The same month he informed Deane he had sent copies of the account to the Superintendent of Finance. He enclosed a copy. Several months later Morris forwarded the accounts with Barclay's statement to the president of Congress for action.[13]

By order of Congress an auditor had gone over the accounts minutely. This report awaited final approval. It was then sent to the Treasury Board. Congress did not act, and the accounts remained in a suspended state.

Deane abandoned hope. In June 1789 he made a final appeal to John Jay and George Washington, requesting their personal intervention in the settlement of his accounts which had lain dormant for so long. He wrote he was extremely solicitous to have his accounts examined and settled. He never expected to receive any money but wanted his friends and family to know he had not merited the treatment he had received.[14] Jay and Washington ignored this appeal.

The key to congressional inaction lay, of course, in the cloud of suspicion and distrust that now surrounded Deane. The atmosphere was evident even to Deane. He commented sadly to Franklin in October 1783: "I have found by experience that from the moment a man becomes unpopular every report which any way tends to his prejudice is but too readily credited without the least examination or proof, and that for him to attempt to contradict them in public is like an attack on the hydra; for every falsehood detected any calumny obviated several new ones of the same family come forward."[15]

Deane continued to refute inaccurate press reports. He wrote Robert Morris: "The newspaper writers of this country are as mischievously busy as those of ours. Since my arrival I have been made by them to visit the Duke of Portland, Lord North, Mr. Fox, and to be intimate with General Arnold, to have furnished Lord Sheffield with a pamphlet on American commerce, &c. I can only assure you, and I have no interest to deceive you, that there is not the least foundation in truth for any of these reports, but that I have lived since my being in London in such obscurity that I have no acquaintance in it, except of some private individuals."[16]

One of the most devastating rumors was that he was associating with Benedict Arnold, and publicly defended Arnold's treason. Arnold, for reasons best known to himself, attempted to renew their old friendship. His advances caused Deane a great deal of embarrassment. The meetings with Arnold appeared as proof of apostasy.

Deane's account of his meetings with Arnold in London varies somewhat from the accounts that circulated in America. His public statement was that while he held no brief for Arnold's conduct, he had roundly denounced Arnold's enemies who, he felt, had "improved every circumstance and accident of his life to push him into desperate measures."[17] The day after arrival in London, General Arnold appeared in Deane's chamber. The landlord opened the door and announced him. Deane was overwhelmed with surprise. Several gentlemen were present, including a Mr. Hodge of Philadelphia. Their reception of Arnold was cold. After a few questions and mutual polite comments, Arnold took leave. On departing he invited, even urged, Deane to dine with him. The invitation was refused. Although Deane changed lodgings the next day, Arnold repeatedly sent invitations. A second, equally unceremonious, visit occurred in Deane's new lodgings. Again a visitor from America was with Deane and remained until Arnold had left. Deane's frankness with Arnold, as the latter departed, was clear. He informed Arnold that visits were disagreeable; that he could not return them, except that he might call with Mr. Sebor some evening to pay respects to Mrs. Arnold, from whom he had received many civilities in Philadelphia. This they did a few evenings later, and Deane did not see Arnold again except on the street.[18]

Both in America and England, people generally believed that Deane and Arnold continued to be friends; John Jay therefore repudiated his friendship with Deane. Jay was "out" when Deane called, and never bothered to answer the card left. From Chaillot in France, Jay expressed his feelings in no uncertain terms: "You are either exceedingly injured or you are no friend to America; and while doubts remain on that point all connexion between us must be suspended. . . . I was told by more than one, on whose information I thought I could rely, that you received visits from, and was on terms of familiarity with, General Arnold. Every American who gives his hand to that man, in my opinion, pollutes it."[19] Thus, in January 1784 ended a friendship that began in the days of the First Continental Congress. Deane in desperation appealed to Jay as late as June 1789, requesting him to use his influence to settle the old matter of the accounts. He hoped for a flicker of the old friendship when a Mr. Sayre mentioned that Jay had inquired after him and expressed a wish for his return. But Jay did not answer Deane's letter.

Another rumor in America was that Deane was in the confidence of the ministry and adviser on American affairs. The result of such advice was assumed. While in Belgium, Deane had met Andrew Allen, a friend of Lord Shelburne, who had been impressed by Deane's knowledge of American affairs and desire to re-establish Anglo-American trade.[20] Allen recommended Deane to Shelburne as adviser on American affairs. Shelburne's correspondence indicates initial acceptance of Allen's suggestion. But upon reflection, Shelburne apparently decided that because of his reputation Deane would be unacceptable in the settlement of 1783.[21]

Almost from the time of his arrival in London, Deane supposedly urged an anti-American commercial policy upon the British. The basis for this

[113]

rumor was a pamphlet by Lord Sheffield describing his conversations with Deane. The latter maintained that views in the publication were the exact opposite of what he had told Sheffield. His acquaintance with Sheffield was accidental, and he had no knowledge of Sheffield's political character nor of his intention of writing on American commerce. He had answered his lordship's queries straightforwardly. He had few acquaintances in London, and polite attention to a stranger naturally had led him to visit Sheffield. He had formed an intimate acquaintance with the family. Deane and Sheffield had many conversations regarding American commerce in the presence of other persons who could testify that Deane's sentiments differed from those in the pamphlet. Sheffield wanted to preserve the Navigation Act; Deane argued that the Act needed alterations.[22]

Deane nonetheless received credit for the undesirable commercial clauses in the treaty of 1783. To his brother Simeon he admitted the futility of combatting the reports: "For though I sent You proofs of the falsity of those reports, strong as those from holy writ, or mathematical demonstration, it would avail nothing in the present Temper of the Times."[23] It now seems preposterous that a poor, distressed, even despised exile should have influenced the councils of a nation. American commerce had been excluded from the British West Indies as well as the British Empire. But Americans in England generally believed that the information and advice Deane had given the British minister was the cause.

Deane was acquainted with only one British minister, Charles James Fox, and in an interview with Fox had discussed "a plan for accommodating the affair of our commerce and intercourse with the British West-Indies, and . . . my reasons in support of it." Fox listened and gave assurance that he would introduce a bill with Deane's commercial ideas.[24]

Deane believed the chief resentment against him stemmed from Lord Sheffield's pamphlet; yet, regardless of consequences of the publication of this pamphlet, Sheffield proved one of the few friends Deane made in England. Sheffield and his family were sincere. During his entire stay in England, Deane was a frequent and welcome guest in the family's London house. In April 1785 his lordship wrote complaining of neglect and expressing hope that a visit to the Sheffield place would soon occur. Illness prevented this visit. The correspondence between the two men revealed mutual regard and admiration. There is little doubt that during Deane's last illness

Sheffield contributed to his support and offered to pay passage to America should Deane desire it.[25]

In the autumn of 1785 Deane's spirits had revived. In October of that year he submitted a plan to the Governor-General of Canada, Lord Dorchester, for a canal from Lake Champlain around the rapids of St. John, into the St. Lawrence River of a certain burthen.[26] Impressed by the plan, Dorchester told the Secretary of State for Foreign Affairs, Lord Sydney, that "as far as a cursory view of the country can justify an opinion, this object appears to be practicable and useful, both in a commercial and political view, provided the conditions of executing the same be not objectionable."[27] Deane submitted the plan to Sydney, and for a time hoped that the government would support it. He proposed that the canal be constructed with government funds and a toll charged for ships. If the minister approved, Deane planned to go to Canada to arrange and prepare whatever was necessary for the plan's execution. The idea of again doing something excited him. If it failed, he would be no worse than at present. The prospect of success in a great undertaking relieved his mind. To his disappointment, the project never received approval.

The final decade of Silas Deane's life was a period of disappointment, when one by one he saw each plan for relief and recovery fade and wither. The years of frustration took their toll. In 1783 he described his condition: "My circumstances from 1780 to this hour shew that I have been in distress, which everyone who knows me knows that I never was before. Doctor Franklin, Beaumarchais, Monsr. Monthieu, and others, know what my funds have been, and whence obtained for my support, on the very small remains of which subsisting, not living. I have not kept a servant or ventured into a hackney coach, except in a storm, since I have been in this country; such is the economy to which I am forced by my misfortunes."[28]

A glimpse of Deane's life comes from another letter in 1788 to Lord Sheffield. Deane apologized for his failure to write on grounds of weakness. He had been too much affected to write earlier. His fever had been constant and increasing; strength had left him until he was just able to walk his room. He mentioned that he received little rest at night because of almost incessant coughing, night sweats, and chills. Fruit, a poached egg, or an egg beat up in milk warm from the cow, with sugar, nutmeg, and some spirit in it, were his sole nourishment when he was able to take it. His friend and former betrayer, Dr. Bancroft, assisted him financially. Any help at all was cheering.[29]

His physician, Dr. Jefferies, recommended a sea voyage, but Deane felt that under the circumstances this was not wise. To be without fruit, milk, or vegetables, subject to the heat and calms of the passage and the violent equinoctial gales would be severe enough for a man in good health. His body racked with pain and mind "distracted with reflections on the past, present, and probable future," he would not survive. Deane suspected that Jefferies was baffled by his disorder and was sending him to sea to die.[30]

His brothers and friends constantly worried about the reports of his distressed mental state. To his brother Barnabas he related a curious incident of chicanery involving American officials. "I have been confined for the greater part of time, ever since December last to my chamber, by a complication of disorders, occasioned in part, and greatly increased, by the distressed state of my circumstances, which have at times drove me to a state of almost absolute distraction. The assistance of Dr. Bancroft, and of two or three other friends have kept me from perishing, as great part of the time I have scarcely been able to recollect one day what had passed the preceding. In this state advantage was taken, and I was plundered of almost the whole of my cloaths [sic], and many papers of importance."[31]

The man who stole Deane's papers went to Paris and offered them to Thomas Jefferson, the American minister, for one hundred and twenty guineas. If the minister did not want them, they would be offered to the British. Jefferson requested twenty-four hours to examine the books and determine their value. Jefferson reported to John Jay, Secretary of Foreign Affairs, that "one [volume] contained all his accounts with the U. S. from his first coming to Europe, to Jan. 10, 1781. Presuming that the Treasury board was in possession of this account till his arrival in Philadelphia, Aug. 1778 and that he had never given in the subsequent part, I had that subsequent part copied from the book, and now enclose it, as it may on some occasion or other perhaps, be useful in the Treasury office. The other volume contained all his correspondencies from Mar. 30. to Aug. 23, 1777. I had a list of the letters taken, by their dates and addresses, which will enable you to form a general idea of the collection. On perusal of many of them, I thought it desirable that they should not come to the hands of the British minister . . ." Jefferson requested the authority to buy them, as he thought the material worth the price. "Indeed I would have given that sum to cut out a single sentence which contained evidence of a fact not proper to be committed to the hands of enemies."

At the end of the twenty-four-hour period Jefferson surrendered the books because he did not have authorization. The thief-owner returned to London "without making any promise that he would await the event of the orders you might think proper to give."[32] In reply to Jefferson's request to buy Deane's Account and Letter Books, Jay wrote: "I wish you had purchased them. On this Subject I cannot indeed give you any Instructions or Authority; but I will venture to advise you in express Terms to make the Purchase. . ."[33]

A new episode in the case of Deane's stolen papers occurred in March 1789. Jefferson wrote Bancroft in London that he had purchased two volumes of Deane's accounts and correspondence. The seller hinted that Deane had "6. or 8. vols. more, . . . he will try to get them also . . ." Jefferson proposed that Bancroft purchase all remaining volumes: "I think you might venture as far as fifty guineas, and proportionably for fewer . . . I suppose his distresses and his crapulous habits will not render him difficult on this head."[34]

Bancroft's reaction is unknown. It is doubtful that he took the matter up with Deane, but he did answer Jefferson's letter. In March 1789 Jefferson informed Jay that he hoped the business finished. The minister reported that after bargaining he had been able to purchase two volumes for twenty-five louis instead of the original one hundred and twenty. According to his information Deane had no other volumes.[35]

Meanwhile, Deane had toyed with the idea of returning to the United States. Each time the uncertainty of his reception had caused him to postpone the decision. As early as 1783 he had written his brother Simeon of his isolated state: "Calumniated and persecuted in America, in effect proscribed in France, and without friends or patrons in this country, and what is worse, without funds to procure them or to enable me to enter on any business of consequence, I have entertained thoughts of returning to Virginia, . . ." But, Deane continued, he was deterred by the climate and by his ignorance of his countrymen's feelings toward him. "I can by no means think of returning to a country, however dear to me, in which I may be subject to insult or contumely."[36]

[117]

It admittedly would be difficult to return home. From Edward Langworthy in June 1783 Deane received an unvarnished statement of his unpopularity in America:

It is painful for me to mention, & even beyond your imagination to conceive,
how much wicked & malicious Men have endeavored to blacken your Character with your Countrymen. Their persecution has been detestable, & cruel;
but I am confident of your Innocence, and know the Ingratitude, that has been
the reward of your Labors, it has had no Influence on my mind, but rather
increased my esteem & affection for you. I was lately in Philadelphia, & was
pleased, in a conversation with your old friend Pelatiah to find that he still
retained his Esteem for you & spoke kindly of you.[37]

Even Robert Morris, his staunch supporter, was uncertain. In 1785 Morris, in answer to a query, informed Deane that, at first, his reception in
America would be mixed. Beyond a doubt his enemies would keep alive the
resentment created by the publication of the wartime letters. Even so, fear
and hatred against the Tories was disappearing. He warned Deane that
those who judged his conduct as treason might arouse opinion against him
to such an extent that the few who believed him innocent would repudiate
him. "From the hand of time alone can you expect that the impressions
against you will be obliterated."[38]

Not all reactions were unfavorable. In July 1785 Deane heard from Jacob
Sebor of New London, Connecticut: "It gives me great pleasure to hear you
enjoy your health and I had flattered myself you would have taken a Passage
for America this Spring. Your friends in this State ofen enquire after you,
and would be very happy to see you and I can assure you they are not very
few."[39]

In September 1788 Barnabas, Deane's brother, expressed fear that he had
died because he had not written. Barnabas described the reports of Deane's
poor health and circumstances. "Let me Intreat you to Return to this
Country Again you have friends that will keep you from want. You can
Compound your Creditors, they have already taken All The Property you
have in this Country; they can get no more."[40]

During Deane's illness in 1788, as mentioned, Sheffield offered to pay
passage to America. Deane proudly refused. In November of the same year

he received a remonstrance from Winthrop Saltonstall complaining of failure to write, and expressing concern for Deane's illness. Saltonstall continued: "I am exceeding glad at the suggestion of your intention to revisit America; no one will be happier in embracing you in this part of the world than I shall. When at New London I shall be happy in receiving you into my family, and though not with that elegance you have been used to, you can no where receive a more sincere and hearty welcome."[41] In December Barnabas urged more strongly: "Yours in August 10th is just Come to hand and the Contents of which gives me pain Altho' from Reports it was not unexpected, I must beg of you to Leave London, what Can you Expect by Staying there but Beggery & Distress, I have not the Least Expectation of Your Ever doing any kind of Business. Again I Judge from what is Past, I will willingly find a Home for you if you will Come to this Place where I have a good House Partly Built, Your Creditors will not find it to be worth their Attention to put you to Gaol . . ."[42]

Yet Deane postponed the decision to return. For seven years he had lived the life of an exile in England. He had experienced severe physical and mental anguish, apart from friends and family and those who might have assisted in re-establishing his good name.

In August 1789 he decided to return. The cause of this decision is unknown. Reaction was varied but definite. From Paris, Jefferson wrote James Madison: "Silas Deane is coming over to finish his days in America, not having one sou to subsist on elsewhere. He is a wretched monument of the consequences of a departure from right."[43] From London in the same month, Samuel Peters wrote expressing a wish for a speedy passage home. "I Sincerely hope your Zeal, Wisdom & Labours may find a proper Reward in the Gratitude & Justice of Congress and of the American Citizens at large; but should Southern Policy prevail against northern Integrity, and your Merit go on neglected, you will enjoy the Consolation of having been the Savior of the Rights & Liberties of America, & thereby proved yourself a true Son of your pious & patriotic Ancestors, who fought every danger to avoid Persecution, and to turn a Savage World into an Asylum for Religious Virtue & Liberty."[44]

Fate had one more disappointment in store for Silas Deane. He died September 23, 1789, after an illness of four hours, on board a Boston packet homeward bound. The vessel, some four hours out, returned to Deal, where Deane was buried in St. George's Church yard. Deane, fifty-four years old, had met his last disappointment.

The English newspapers noted Deane's death. His obituary notices were, in the main, fair and factual and from the British point of view complimentary. The *Gentleman's Magazine* announced that "He was second to very few politicians in knowledge, plans, designs, and execution; deficient only in placing confidence in his compatriots, and doing them service before he got his compensation of which no wellbred politician was before him ever guilty."[45] The *American Mercury*, in a reprint from a London paper, noted: "Having . . . been accused of embezzling large sums of money intrusted to his care for the purchase of arms and ammunition, Mr. Deane sought an asylum in this country, where his habits of life, at first economical, and afterwards penurious in the extreme, amply refute the malevolence of his enemies."[46]

Deane's death, like the last years of his life, was of little interest to people in America. Congress did not pause in a moment of silence, nor did any orator deem it proper to recall his contribution to the Revolution.

The family's reaction was mixed: some members may have mourned his passing; that others did not regret his death is probable. Simeon, who had declared himself ready to give his life for Deane, was dead. Barnabas, with whom Deane had planned to live, expressed the proper appreciation to Deane's friends in England and paid "the balance of the funeral charges."[47] Jesse, the beloved son, found it necessary to sell his father's gold snuffbox after removing the picture.[48] The sentiments of Samuel Blachley Webb, a stepson, if recorded have not been preserved. Another stepson, Joseph, hearing the news of his stepfather's demise, exclaimed: "The seen [*sic*] with S. D. is closed."[49] Dr. Edward Bancroft, the man who had betrayed Deane in 1776–78 but befriended him in England, characterized him as a Christian gentleman and esteemed his memory.[50]

The death of Silas Deane could be ignored, but his unsettled accounts long stood as a reminder that he could not be forgotten. More than half a century passed before Congress consented to settle this business of the Revolution. In 1840 Deane's heirs once more presented a petition for compensation. On February 17, 1841, the Senate Committee on Revolutionary

Claims reported favorably. On July 27 the Claims Committee of the House of Representatives concurred. Congress granted a claim of thirty-seven thousand dollars on the ground that a former audit was "ex parte, erroneous, and a gross injustice to Silas Deane."[51]

NOTES

Chapter 1

1. *Dictionary of American Biography,* edited by Allen Johnson and Dumas Malone, 34 vols. (New York, 1930), 5:173–75; *The New England Historical and Genealogical Register,* 104 vols. (Boston, 1847– —); "The Deane Papers," *The New York Historical Society Collections,* 5 vols. (New York, 1886–1890), 1:1–14 (hereafter cited as *Deane Papers*); *Elizabeth Kite Manuscript,* No. 27143, Manuscript Division, Library of Congress, Washington D. C. (hereafter cited as *Kite MSS.*).

2. Dean to S. B. Webb, Dec. 6, 1773, *Correspondence and Journals of Samuel Blachley Webb,* ed. Worthington Chauncey Ford, 3 vols. (New York, 1938), 1:15 (hereafter cited as Webb, *Journals*).

3. S. B. Webb to Barnabas Deane, June 12, 1778, *Family Letters of Samuel Blachley Webb, 1764–1807,* ed. Worthington Chauncey Ford (New York, 1912), pp. 71–72 (hereafter cited as Webb, *Family Letters*).

4. Simpson to S. B. Webb, Mar. 29, 1775, Webb, *Family Letters,* p. 13.

5. *Public Records of the Colony of Connecticut, 1636–1776,* edited by James H. Trumbull and Charles J. Hoadly, 15 vols. (Hartford, 1850–1890), 14:94 (hereafter cited as *Connecticut Public Records*).

6. Ibid., 14:412

7. Ibid., 14:161; "Four years previously (1753) a group of Connecticut speculators had organized themselves as the Susquehannah [*sic*] Company and purchased from the Six Nations a large tract of land in the Susquehannah Valley of Pennsylvania. Connecticut claimed this land by virtue of her sea-to-sea charter, and the assembly of that colony gave its sanction to the undertaking. The Penn family, proprietors of Pennsylvania, of course opposed the claim, but the Quaker faction in Philadelphia, led by Joseph Galloway and Benjamin Franklin and in control of the assembly of the province, was at odds with the Penns. This Quaker group now formed a 'Friendly Association' which collected more than four thousand pounds in order to increase its influence among the Indians by means of presents." Thomas Perkins Abernethy, *Western Lands and the American Revolution* (New York, 1937), p. 18.

8. *Connecticut Public Records,* 14:94.

9. Henry Reed Stiles, *The History of Ancient Wethersfield, Connecticut,* 2 vols. (New York, 1904), 1:490–95 (hereafter cited as Stiles, *Wethersfield*).

10. The delegates were elected by the Connecticut Committee of Correspondence. Later the same delegates were elected by the General Assembly of Connecticut, *Connecticut Public Records,* 14:324; *American Archives,* ed. Peter Force, series 4, 6 vols. (Washington, D. C., 1837–1846), 1:554, 854, 895 (hereafter cited as Force, *Archives*).

11. Deane to Mrs. Deane, Aug. 29, Sept. 8, 1874, *Collections of the Connecticut Historical Society,* ed. J. Hammond Trumbull (Hartford, 1870), 2:143–46, 163–76 (hereafter cited as Deane, *Correspondence*).

12. Edward C. Burnett, *The Continental Congress* (New York, 1941), p. 24: Deane to Mrs. Deane, Aug. 29, 1774, Deane, *Correspondence,* 2:145.

13. "Silas Deane on Relief for Boston," June 1774–?, Webb, *Journals,* 1:30–32.

14. Deane to Mrs. Deane, June 16, 1775, Deane, *Correspondence,* 2:264–65.

15. *Journals of the Continental Congress,* ed. Worthington Chauncey Ford, 34 vols. (Washington, D. C., 1905–1937), 2:67, 102–3 (hereafter cited as *Journals of Congress*).

16. Ibid., 3:378.

17. Ibid., 2:90.

18. Ibid., 2:234–35.

19. Ibid., 3:492.

20. Deane to Mrs. Deane, June 3, June 18, Oct. 17, 1775, Deane, *Correspondence,* 2:266–68, 252–56, 312; see also "Diary" (1775–1776), Deane Manuscript, Connecticut Historical Society (Hartford) (hereafter cited as *Deane MSS.,* CHS).

21. Deane to Mrs. Deane, July 20, Sept. 22, Oct. 2, 1775, Deane, *Correspondence,* 2:289–93, 307, 308.

22. Deane to Mrs. Deane, Nov. 26, 1775, ibid., 2:324.

23. Mumford to Deane, Jan. 10, 1776, *Deane MSS.,* CHS; Trumbull to Deane, Oct. 20, 1775, *Deane Papers,* 1:86.

24. James Hogg to Colonel Robert Henderson, Dec. 22, 1775, Force, *Archives,* 4:543–45.

25. Samuel Adams to James Warren, July 1, 1778, *The Writings of Samuel Adams,* ed. Henry A. Cushing, 4 vols. (New York, 1904), 4:47 (hereafter cited as Adams, *Writings*).

26. Deane to Mrs. Deane, Jan. 21, 1776, Deane, *Correspondence,* 2:350.

27. Nov. 29, 1775, *Secret Journals* [of Congress, May 10, 1775 to Oct. 26, 1787] Roll No. 19, Reel 1, *Papers of the Continental Congress,* National Archives, Washington, D. C. (hereafter cited as *P. C. C.*)

28. Committee of Secret Correspondence to Arthur Lee, Dec. 12, 1775, U. S. Department of State, *The Revolutionary Diplomatic Correspondence of the United States,* ed. Francis Wharton, 6 vols. (Washington, D. C., 1889, 2:63 (hereafter cited as Wharton, *Diplomatic Correspondence*).

29. Deane to Mrs. Deane, Mar. 3, 1776, Deane, *Correspondence,* 2:360–63.

30. Committee of Secret Correspondence to Deane, Mar. 3, 1776, Wharton, *Diplomatic Correspondence,* 2:78–80.

31. "Correspondence between Silas Deane and his brothers and their business and political associates, 1771–1795," *Collections of the Connecticut Historical Society* (Hartford, 1930), 23:19.

32. Committee of Secret Correspondence to Deane, Mar. 3, 1776, Wharton, *Diplomatic Correspondence,* 2:78; Benjamin Franklin to Edward Bancroft, Mar. 22, 1776, *Deane Papers,* 1:127–28; Deane to Mrs. Deane, [?] Mar. 3, 1776, Deane, *Correspondence,* 2:363; *The Diary and Autobiography of John Adams,* ed. L. H. Butterfield, 4 vols. (Cambridge, Mass., 1961), 3:339–41.

Chapter 2

1. Committee of Secret Correspondence to Deane, Mar. 3, 1776, Wharton, *Diplomatic Correspondence,* 2:78–79.

2. Deane to Dumas, Aug. 18, 1776, Wharton, *Diplomatic Correspondence,* 2:128.

3. Committee of Secret Correspondence, Aug. 18, 1776, Wharton, *Diplomatic Correspondence,* 2:124; "I do not recollect whether Mr. Deane had arrived in France before 10 of June 1776, but from his great want of money when I joined him a few months later, I hardly think it [the lost million] could have been paid him," Benjamin Franklin to Charles Thomas, 1777, *P. C. C.,* pp. 100–206.

4. Committee of Secret Correspondence to Deane, Mar. 3, 1776, Wharton, *Diplomatic Correspondence,* 2:78–79.

5. Deane to Committee of Secret Correspondence, Aug. 15, 1776, ibid., 2:123.

6. Beaumarchais to Vergennes, Aug. 13, 1776, *Facsimiles of Manuscripts relating to America in the Archives of Europe, 1773–1788,* ed., Benjamin Franklin Stevens, 24 vols. (London, 1870–1902), No. 889 (hereafter cited as *Facsimiles*).

7. Deane to Committee of Secret Correspondence, Aug. 18, 1776, Wharton, *Diplomatic Correspondence*, 2:116.

8. James Rochford to Lord Shelburne, Jan. 7, 1767, *Shelburne Papers*, 38:94, Clements Library, Ann Arbor, Mich.; John Durand, "Bonvouloir," *New Materials for the History of the American Revolution taken from Documents in the French Archives* (New York, 1889), pp. 2–16 (hereafter cited as *New Materials*).

9. Durand, "Beaumarchais," *New Materials*, pp. 87–103; George Clinton Genet, contributor, "Beaumarchais' Plan to Aid the Colonies," *Magazine of American History*, 2a (1878):671–72; John J. Meng, "A Footnote to Secret Aid in the American Revolution," *American Historical Review* 43 (1938):791–95.

10. Elizabeth S. Kite, "How the Declaration of Independence Reached Europe," *Daughters of the American Revolution Magazine:* 62, no. 7 (July 1928): 405–413; Henry Doniol, *Histoire de la Participation, à l'établissement des États-Unis d'Amérique*, 6 vols. (Paris, 1884–1893), 1:664 (hereafter cited as Doniol, *France and the Revolution*).

11. Edward Bancroft, *A Narrative of the Objects and Proceedings of Silas Deane, Commissioner of the United Colonies to France; made to the British in 1776*, ed. Paul Leicester Ford (Brooklyn, 1891); see also Beaumarchais to Deane, 10 letters July 18, 1776, to Feb. 4, 1778, No. 18, Record Group 39, Records of the Bureau of Accounts (Treasury), Fiscal Section, National Archives.

12. Deane to Committee of Secret Correspondence, Aug. 18, 1776, *Deane Papers*, 1:195–218.

13. Deane to Jay, Dec. 3, 1776, Wharton, *Diplomatic Correspondence*, 2:212–16.

14. Deane to Beaumarchais, July 20, 1776, ibid., 2:102.

15. Beaumarchais to Deane, July 22, 1776, *Deane MSS.*, CHS.

16. Ibid.

17. Committee of Secret Correspondence to Deane, Mar. 3, 1776, Wharton, *Diplomatic Correspondence*, 2:79.

18. Deane to Committee of Secret Correspondence, Aug. 18, 1776, ibid., 2:120.

19. (Beaumarchais) R. Hortalez and Co. to Committee of Secret Correspondence, Aug. 18, 1776, ibid, 2:130.

20. Arthur Lee to Committee of Secret Correspondence, Dec. 31, 1776, ibid, 2:242; Deane to Beaumarchais, Mar. 29, 1778, *Deane Papers*, 2:438–40; De Francey to Beaumarchais, July 31, 1778, Theveneau De Francey, *Beaumar-*

chais the Merchant: Letters of Theveneau de Francey, 1777–1780, ed. John Bigelow (New York, 1870), p. 9.

21. Du Bourg to Vergennes, July 13, 1776, Stevens, *Facsimiles,* No. 881; Deane to Committee of Secret Correspondence, Aug. 18, 1776, Wharton, *Diplomatic Correspondence,* 2:113–16.

22. (Beaumarchais) R. Hortalez and Co. to Committee of Secret Correspondence, Aug. 18, 1776, ibid., 2:131.

23. Friedrich Kapp, *The Life of John Kalb* (New York, 1884), p. 84.

24. Deane to Committee of Secret Correspondence, Oct. 1, 1776, Wharton, *Diplomatic Correspondence,* 2:153; Beaumarchais to Vergennes, January 30, 1777, Stevens, *Facsimiles,* No. 916; Elizabeth S. Kite, "Lafayette and His Companions on the 'Victoire'," *Records of the American Catholic Historical Society,* 45, no. 1 (Mar. 1934).

25. Beaumarchais to Deane, Oct. 14, 1776, *Deane MSS.,* CHS.

26. Deane to Robert Morris, Dec. 14, 1776, ibid.; Deane to Committee of Secret Correspondence, Aug. 18, Oct. 1, 1776, Deane to William Bingham, Oct. 17, 1776, Deane to Committee of Secret Correspondence, Nov. 9, 1776, Wharton, *Diplomatic Correspondence,* 2:120, 153, 173, 192; Deane to Secret Committee of Correspondence, Nov. 28, 1776, *Deane Papers,* 1:371–78.

27. Deane to Jay, Dec. 3, 1776, John Jay, *The Correspondence and Public Papers,* ed. Henry P. Johnson, 4 vols (New York, 1890), 1:97–102; see also Wharton, *Diplomatic Correspondence,* 2:212–16.

28. Morris to Deane, Jan. 11, 1777, *Deane MSS.,* CHS.

29. Stevens, *Facsimiles,* No. 235; Margaret Miller, "The Spy Activities of Dr. Edward Bancroft," *Journal of Modern History* 22 (1928): 70–77; 157–70.

30. Dr. B[ancroft] to Mr. W[entworth], Apr. 24, 1777, "Statement concerning the Employment of Lt. Col. Edward Smith with regards to Capt. Hynson and a sketch of the information obtained, end of March, 1777"; Paul Wentworth to William Eden, Dec. 28, 1777, Stevens, *Facsimiles,* Nos. 65, 248; Lee, *Life of Arthur Lee,* 1:366. Some doubt as to the effectiveness of Bancroft's role as a British agent is noted in Richard W. Van Alstyne, "Great Britain, the War for Independence, and the 'Gathering Storm' in Europe, 1775–1778," *Huntington Library Quarterly* 27 (1964): 311–46. An evaluation of Bancroft as a man of science may be found in C. A. Browne, "A Sketch of the Life and Chemical Theories of Dr. Edward Bancroft," *Journal of Chemical Education* 14 (March 1937): 103–7.

31. Arthur Lee to Committee of Secret Correspondence, Apr. 26, 1778, Wharton, *Diplomatic Correspondence,* 2:562; Archibald B. Shepperson, "Public

Enemy and Private Friend," *John Paradise and Lucy Ludwell* (Richmond, 1942), pp. 351–79; Margaret Miller, "The Spy Activities of Dr. Edward Bancroft," *Journal of Modern History* 22 (1928): 70–77, 157–70.

32. Deane to Committee of Secret Correspondence, Aug. 18, 1776, Wharton, *Diplomatic Correspondence,* 2:124.

33. George Lupton to William Eden, June 4, 1777, Stevens, *Facsimiles,* No. 168; Richard B. Morris, *The Peacemakers: The Great Powers and American Independence* (New York, 1956).

34. George Lupton to William Eden, Apr. 30, May 7, July 9, 1777, Stevens, *Facsimiles,* Nos. 147, 154, 179.

35. Lupton to William Eden, October 15, 1777, ibid., No. 204.

36. Lupton to William Eden, May 28, 1777, ibid., No. 162.

37. *Ibid.*

38. Lupton to William Eden, Aug. 20, 1777, ibid., No. 187.

39. Deane to Dumas, Dec. 1776, Wharton, *Diplomatic Correspondence,* 2:225.

40. Ibid.

41. Deane to Dumas, Aug. 18, 1776, *Deane Papers,* 1:220.

42. Deane to Dumas, June 7, 1777, Wharton, *Diplomatic Correspondence,* 2:-331–32.

43. Ibid.

44. "Memoire Secret pour les Ministers du Roi, Seuls," Mar. 13, 1778, translation, *Deane Papers,* 2:403.

45. Deane to John Jay, Dec. 3, 1776, Jay, *Correspondence and Public Papers,* 1:102; Deane to Secret Committee of Correspondence, Aug. 18, 1776, Wharton, *Diplomatic Correspondence,* 2:127.

46. Deane to Committee of Secret Correspondence, Aug. 8, 1776, Wharton, *Diplomatic Correspondence,* 2:127; Elizabeth S. Kite, "Lafayette and His Companions on the 'Victoire'," *Records of the American Catholic Historical Society* 45(1) (March 1934):1–32.

47. De Kalb to Deane (enclosure), Dec. 17, 1776, *Deane Papers,* 1:427–31.

48. De Francey, *Letters,* p. 5; Deane to Robert Morris, Sept. 23, 1777, Miscellany Folder 104, No. 2827, *Papers of the Continental Congress,* Manuscript Division, Library of Congress.

49. Edward Bancroft to Deane, Feb. [?] 1777, Deane to Robert Morris, Mar. 16, 1777, *Deane Papers,* 2:4, 24, 30–31; William Clark Bell, "John the

Painter," *Pennsylvania Magazine of History and Biography* 68 (1939):1–23; Deane to Vergennes, Mar. 22, 1777, Stevens, *Facsimiles,* No. 664.

50. George Lupton to William Eden, May 22, 1777, Stevens, *Facsimiles,* No. 696.

51. M. Favier to Vergennes, Jan. 2, 1778, ibid., No. 1818.

52. Ibid.

53. Lord Stormont to Lord Weymouth, Dec. 25, 1776, ibid., No. 1402; Thomas Hutchinson, *The Diary and Letters of His Excellency, Thomas Hutchinson,* ed. Peter Orlando Hutchinson (Boston, 1884), 2:140–144.

54. Chaumont to Vergennes, Apr. 18, 1778, *Affaires Étrangeres Correspondence Politique, États-Unis,* Manuscript Division, Library of Congress, 1, no. 98 (hereafter cited as *Political Correspondence, États-Unis*).

Chapter 3

1. Deane to Committee of Secret Correspondence, Nov. 6, 1776, Wharton, *Diplomatic Correspondence,* 2:190.

2. Franklin to Joseph Priestly, July 7, 1775, *The Writings of Benjamin Franklin,* ed. Albert H. Smyth, 10 vols. (New York, 1907), 6:409.

3. *Journals of Congress,* 4:62, 159 n., 172; 6:1071–72; John Adams, *The Works of John Adams, Second President of the United States,* ed. Charles Francis Adams, 10 vols. (Boston, 1850), 3:29; see entry for Feb. 16, 1776, Butterfield, *Diary of John Adams,* 2:229–30.

4. Thomas Paine, *The Complete Writings of Thomas Paine,* ed. Philip S. Foner, 2 vols. (New York, 1945), 1:21; Henry Leffmann, "The Real Thomas Paine, Patriot and Publicist, A Philosopher Misunderstood," *Pennsylvania Magazine of History and Biography* 46 (1922): 81–100.

5. Adams, *Works,* 2:510–17; Butterfield, *Diary of John Adams,* 3:327–30.

6. *Journals of Congress,* 5:425.

7. Adams, *Works,* 2:516; Butterfield, *Diary of John Adams,* 3:327–30.

8. Adams, *Works,* 2:516.

9. Edward E. Hale and Edward E. Hale, Jr., *Franklin in Paris,* 2 vols. (Boston, 1887), 1:77; Stormont to Weymouth, Dec. 25, 1776, Stevens, *Facsimiles,* No. 1402.

10. Wharton, *Diplomatic Correspondence,* 1:145.

11. Butterfield, *Diary of John Adams,* 2:347.

12. Beaumarchais to Vergennes, Dec. 7, 1777, Stevens, *Facsimiles,* No. 1763.

13. Deane to Jonathan Williams, Jan. 13, 1778, *Deane Papers,* 2:327.

14. *Journals of Congress,* 13:367; Arthur Lee to Committee of Foreign Affairs, June 1, 1778, Wharton, *Diplomatic Correspondence,* 2:600–3; Irving Brant, *James Madison: The Nationalist, 1780–1787* (Indianapolis, 1948), pp. 58–69; Frederick R. Kirland, "Jefferson and Franklin," *Pennsylvania Magazine of History and Biography* 71 (1947): 218–22.

15. Franklin and Deane to Committee of Secret Correspondence, Mar. 12, 1777, Wharton, *Diplomatic Correspondence,* 2:284–85.

16. Deane to Beaumarchais, Jan. 6, 1777, *Deane Papers,* 1:449.

17. Franklin, Deane, and Lee to Vergennes, Jan. 5; commissioners in Paris to Committee of Secret Correspondence, Jan. 17; Deane to Committee of Secret Correspondence, Jan. 20, 1777, Wharton, *Diplomatic Correspondence,* 2:245, 248, 252.

Chapter 4

1. Commissioners in Paris to Committee of Secret Correspondence, Jan. 17, 1777, Wharton, *Diplomatic Correspondence,* 2:249.

2. Vergennes to Noailles, July 26; Stormont to Weymouth, June 18, 1777, Stevens, *Facsimiles,* Nos. 1590, 1551; Vergennes to commissioners in Paris, July 16; Franklin and Deane to Vergennes, July 17, 1777, Wharton, *Diplomatic Correspondence,* 2:364–65, 365–66; consult index in Stevens, under Conyngham, Wickes, *Dolphin, Lexington,* and *Reprisal;* see also Vergennes to commissioners in Paris, Mar. 2, 1777, *P. C. C.,* pp. 102–62, 123–6–59.

3. Corwin, *French Policy and the American Alliance,* p. 100; Deane to Robert Morris, May 26, 1777, Samuel F. Henkels, *The Confidential Correspondence of Robert Morris* (Philadelphia, 1917), no. 129, p. 64.

4. Deane to Robert Morris, Apr. 11, May 26, 1777, Henkels, *Confidential Correspondence,* No. 126, p. 63, No. 129, p. 64.

5. Deane to Robert Morris, Aug. 23, 1777, Wharton, *Diplomatic Correspondence,* 2:381.

6. Lenoir to Vergennes, Aug. 11; M. Amelot to Vergennes, Sept. 24, 1777, Stevens, *Facsimiles,* Nos. 1647, 1694.

7. Arthur Lee to Samuel Adams, Sept. 9, 1777, Richard Henry Lee, *Life of Arthur Lee,* 2:111.

8. William Lee to R. H. Lee, Nov. 30, 1777, William Lee, *Letters of William Lee, 1766–1783,* ed. Worthington Chauncey Ford (New York, 1891), 1:-279–80 (hereafter cited as *Letters*); Arthur Lee to Samuel Adams, Sept. 9, 1777, R. H. Lee, *Life of Arthur Lee,* 2:111.

9. William Lee to R. H. Lee, Nov. 24, 1777, *Life of Arthur Lee,* 2:267–71; see also 1:340–43, 346, 376.

10. Robert Morris to Henry Laurens, Dec. 26; Arthur Lee to R. H. Lee, Mar. 6, 1777, *Deane Papers,* 2:245–54, 21–22; see also *Lee MSS.,* Harvard University.

11. *Deane Papers,* 2:87–88; *Papers in Relation to the Case of Silas Deane Now Published from the Original Manuscript,* ed. Edward Duncan Ingraham (Philadelphia, 1855), p. 200.

12. John Ross to Deane, July 22, 1777, *Deane Papers,* 2:97.

13. William Lee to Deane, Aug. 12, 1777, William Lee, *Letters,* 1:215.

14. William Lee to Francis Lightfoot Lee, Nov. 11, 1777; William Lee to R. H. Lee, Nov. 24, 1777, ibid., 1:264, 271.

15. William Lee to Francis Lightfoot Lee, Nov. 11, 1777, ibid., 1:264.

16. Franklin to Jonathan Williams, Dec. 22, 1777, *The Complete Works of Benjamin Franklin,* ed. John Begelow, 10 vols. (New York, 1887), 1:343.

17. Deane to Morris, Sept. 23, 1777, *Deane Papers,* 2:146–50.

18. William Lee to Francis Lightfoot Lee, Feb. 17, 1778, *Deane Papers,* 2:-368–70; see also *Lee MSS.,* Harvard University.

19. Ross to Deane, Mar. 3, 1778, *Deane Papers,* 2:386.

20. Deane to William Lee, Mar. 11, 1778, ibid., 2:391–92.

21. Deane to Ross, Mar. 15, 1778, ibid., 2:409.

22. Theveneau de Francey, *Letters,* p. 4.

23. Deane to Committee on Foreign Affairs, Sept. 3, 1777; Deane to Committee on Secret Correspondence, Nov. 29, 1776, Wharton, *Diplomatic Correspondence,* 2:387, 201.

24. R. H. Lee, *Life of Arthur Lee,* 1:365, 375, 395; Franklin, Deane, and Lee to Messrs. Berard Freses, Dec. 24, 1777; Franklin, Deane, and Lee to Committee on Foreign Affairs, Feb. 16, 1778, Wharton, *Diplomatic Correspondence,* 2:459, 496.

25. Beaumarchais to Vergennes, Mar. 30, 1777, Stevens, *Facsimiles,* No. 1500.

26. Deane to Harrison, Oct. 5, 1777, *Deane Papers,* 2:172.

27. Deane to Morris, Jan. 4, 1778, ibid., 2:307.

28. Deane to Ross, Mar. 23, 1778, ibid., 2:422.

29. Deane to William Lee, Mar. 11, 1778, ibid., 2:392.

30. Deane to Beaumarchais, Jan. 8, 1777; Beaumarchais to Deane, Feb. 19, 1777, ibid., 1:451, 491.

31. Deane to Jonathan Williams, Oct. 14; Deane to Geradot and Halber, Jan. 8, 1778, ibid., 2:189, 310.

32. Deane to George Washington, Aug. 12, 1778, Wharton, *Diplomatic Correspondence*, 2:680–81.

33. Arthur Lee to R. H. Lee, intercepted, Oct. 4, 1777, Stevens, *Facsimiles*, No. 269.

34. R. H. Lee, *Life of Arthur Lee*, 1:170–71; Arthur Lee to R. H. Lee, Oct. 4, 1777, ibid., 1:114–16.

35. Burton J. Hendrick, "America's First Ambassador," "Arthur Lee, the Volunteer Diplomat," and "Worse than Arnold," *Atlantic* 156 (1935):- 137–48, 316–23, 383–93; Arthur Lee to Theodoric Bland, Dec. 13, 1778, R. H. Lee, *Life of Arthur Lee*, 1:161–62.

36. Arthur Lee to Adams, Sept. 9, 1777, *Life of Arthur Lee*, 2:111.

37. Arthur Lee to R. H. Lee, Oct. 4, 1777, ibid., 2:115.

38. Arthur Lee to R. H. Lee, Jan. 9, 1778, ibid., 2:127–28.

39. Arthur Lee to Adams, Nov. 25, 1777, ibid., 2:124.

40. Bolton (William Carmichael) to M. Jean Tourville, intercepted by the London General Post Office, Nov. 1, 1777, Stevens, *Facsimiles*, No. 288.

41. Deane to Arthur Lee, Dec. 13, 1777, *Deane Papers*, 2:272–73.

Chapter 5

1. Jonathan Loring Austin, the courier selected to carry the news of Burgoyne's surrender to France, sailed from Long Wharf in Boston on Oct. 31. He landed in Nantes on Sunday, Nov. 30, where he stayed with the commercial agent, Mr. Jonathan Williams. On Thursday Austin arrived at Versailles where he spent an hour visiting the Palace before going to Passy to deliver the "Great News." Austin's *Journal* gives a vivid description and dramatic account of his arrival. His "carriage dashed into the courtyard of the Hôtel Balentinois and Franklin and all the Commissioners came down to meet him. 'Sir, is Philadelphia taken?' cried Dr. Franklin to the messen-

ger. 'It is, Sir,' said Austin, and the old man turned away. 'But, Sir, I have greater news than that. General Burgoyne and his whole army are prisoners of war.'" Hale, *Franklin in France*, 1:159.

2. Vergennes to Montmorier, Dec. 13, 1777, Stevens, *Facsimiles*, No. 1775.

3. Stevens, *Facsimiles*, Nos. 277, 288; David Jayne Hill, "A Missing Chapter of Franco-American History," *American Historical Review*, 21 (1916): 712.

4. Lord North to William Eden, Nov. 4, *Auckland Papers*, British Museum Additional Manuscripts 34414, pp. 309–10, General Library, University of Michigan (hereafter cited as *Add. MSS.*); Alan Brown, "William Eden and the American Revolution," Ph.D. thesis, Film No. 1537, University of Michigan; Alan Brown, "The British Peace Offer of 1778: A Study in Ministerial Confusion," *Papers of the Michigan Academy of Science, Arts and Letters*, 40 (1955–1956).

5. Lord Germain to William Eden, Dec. 3, 1777, *Add. MSS.* 34414, p. 391.

6. Bolton (William Carmichael) to M. Jean Tourville, Nov. 1, 1777, Stevens, *Facsimiles*, No. 288.

7. Lupton to William Eden, July 9, 1777, ibid., No. 179.

8. Wentworth to Deane, Dec. 12, 1777, ibid., No. 719.

9. Ibid., No. 719.

10. Wentworth to William Eden, Dec. 17, 1777, *Add. MSS.* 34414, pp. 433–43.

11. R. H. Lee, *Life of Arthur Lee*, 1:366.

12. Ibid., 1:367.

13. Lewis Einstein, *Divided Loyalties: American in England During the War of Independence* (London, 1930), p. 32.

14. Lord North to Eden, Dec. 23, 1777, *Add. MSS.* 34414, pp. 461–62.

15. Lord North to George III, Dec. 23, 1777, *The Correspondence of George III with Lord North from 1760–1783*, ed. Sir John Fortescue, 6 vols. (London, 1927), 3 (no. 2119): 519.

16. "Gérard: Narrative of a Conference with the American Commissioners," Jan. 9, 1778, Stevens, *Facsimiles*, No. 1831; "Some Accounts of James Hutton's Visit to Franklin in France, in December of 1777," *Pennsylvania Magazine of History and Biography* 32 (1908):223–32.

17. Gérard: "Narrative," Stevens, *Facsimiles*, No. 1831.

18. *Treaties and Other International Acts of the United States of America*, ed. Hunter Miller, 7 vols. (Washington, D.C., 1931), 2:38, 42.

19. Arthur Lee to Ralph Izard, Jan. 28, 1778, Wharton, *Diplomatic Correspondence,* 2:477.

20. Ibid.; R. H. Lee, *Life of Arthur Lee,* 1:390–91.

Chapter 6

1. Lovell to Deane, Dec. 8, 1777, Wharton, *Diplomatic Correspondence,* 2:444; *Journals of Congress,* 8:605 n., 946, 1008.

2. Deane to Ross, Jan. 3, 1778, *Deane Papers,* 2:303.

3. Deane to Ross, Mar. 23, 1778, ibid., 2:422.

4. Deane to Jonathan Williams, Mar. 21: Deane to Beaumarchais, Mar. 29, 1778, ibid., 2:420–21, 439.

5. Vergennes to Louis XVI, Jan. 7, 1778, Stevens, *Facsimiles,* No. 1824.

6. "Memoire Secret Pour les Ministres du Roi, Seuls," by Beaumarchais, Mar. 13, 1778, *Deane Papers,* 2:399–406 (translation).

7. Franklin to president of Congress, Mar. 31; Vergennes to president of Congress, Mar. 25, 1778, Silas Deane, *An Address to the United States of North America,* J. Debrett (printer) (London, 1784), Appendices 3, 1.

8. Beaumarchais to Congress, Mar. 18, 1778, *Deane Papers,* 2:429–34.

9. Deane to Beaumarchais, Mar. 29, 1778, *Deane Papers,* 2:439.

10. Arthur Lee to Franklin and Deane, Mar. 31, 1778, Wharton, *Diplomatic Correspondence,* 2:530.

11. Franklin to Arthur Lee, Apr. 1, 1778, ibid., 2:530.

12. Franklin to Arthur Lee, Apr. 4, 1778, ibid., 2:537–41.

13. Ibid., 2:540.

14. Hale, *Franklin in Paris,* 1:459.

15. R. H. Lee to Samuel Adams, Nov. 23, 1777, *Letters of Members of the Continental Congress,* ed. Edmund C. Burnett 6 vols. (Washington, D.C., 1921–33), 2:568 (hereafter cited as Burnett, *Letters of Congress.*)

16. William Lee to Arthur Lee, Apr. 23, June 10, 1778, William Lee, *Letters,* 2:418, 444–45.

17. Adams to McCreary, Sept. 25, 1778, Hale, *Franklin in Paris,* 1:232.

18. Adams to Lovell, July 26, 1778, Wharton, *Diplomatic Correspondence,* 2:664.

'19. Adams to R. H. Lee, Aug. 5, 1778, ibid., 2:678.

20. Izard to Lloyd, Nov. 12, 1777, Ralph Izard, *Correspondence of Ralph Izard of South Carolina from the year 1774 to 1804: With a Short Memoir,* ed. Anne Izard Deas (New York, 1884), p. 379.

21. Lloyd to Izard, Nov. 20, ibid., p. 384; Izard to Henry Laurens, Dec. 21, 1777, "Ralph Izard-Henry Laurens Correspondence," *The South Carolina Historical and Genealogical Magazine* 21–22 (1920–21):49.

22. William Lee to R. H. Lee, Jan. 9, 1778, William Lee, *Letters,* 1:334.

23. William Lee to Arthur Lee, Apr. 23, 1778, ibid., 2:418.

24. R. H. Lee to Samuel Adams, Nov. 23, 1777; R. H. Lee to Henry Laurens, Dec. 26, 1778, R. H. Lee, *Letters,* 1:352, 462; *Journals of Congress,* Nov. 21, 1777, 9:975.

25. Franklin to Lovell, Dec. 21, 1777, Wharton, *Diplomatic Correspondence,* 2:457–58.

26. Franklin to Lovell, July 22, 1778, ibid., 2:656.

27. Lovell to Trumbull, June 30, 1777, Burnett, *Letters of Congress,* 2:394; see also *Joseph Trumbull Papers,* CSL.

28. Lovell to Whipple, June 30, 1777, Burnett, *Letters of Congress,* 2:394.

29. Eliphalet Dyer to Trumbull, July 7, 1777, ibid., 2:405; see also *Joseph Trumbull Papers,* CSL.

30. Lovell to Whipple, July 29, 1777, Burnett, *Letters of Congress,* 2:431.

31. Laurens to John Lewis Gervais, Aug. 5, 1778, ibid., 2:438–39.

32. Laurens to Rutledge, Aug. 12, 1777, ibid., 2:445.

33. Lovell to Wolcott, Aug. 21, 1777, ibid., 2:460; see also *Oliver Wolcott Papers,* CHS.

34. *Journals of Congress,* 8:721.

35. Williams to Trumbull, Nov. 28, 1777, Burnett, *Letters of Congress,* 2:574–75.

36. Lovell to R. H. Lee, Dec. 8, 1777, ibid., 2:581–82.

37. Lovell to Deane, Dec. 8, 1777, Wharton, *Diplomatic Correspondence,* 2:444.

38. "William Duer's Address, with Thomas Paine's Reply," *Deane Papers,* 3:336.

Chapter 7

1. R. H. Lee to Arthur Lee, May 12, May 19, 1778, R. H. Lee, *Letters,* 1:403; 2:408.

2. William Lee to R. H. Lee, Feb. 10, 1779, William Lee, *Letters,* 2:519–23.

3. Deane to John Jay, May 22, 1779, *Deane Papers,* 3:457.

4. Deane to Laurens, July 10, 1778, Wharton, *Diplomatic Correspondence,* 2:643.

5. *Pennsylvania Packet,* July 14, 1778.

6. Deane to president of Congress, July 28, 1778, Wharton, *Diplomatic Correspondence,* 2:668.

7. Deane to Washington, Aug. 12, 1778, ibid., 2:681.

8. Deane to Hancock, Sept. 14, 1778, *Ferdinand J. D. Dreer Collection,* Pennsylvania Historical Society Collection, Philadelphia.

9. *Journals of Congress,* 12:927; see also "Information Given to Congress by Richard Henry Lee, Sept. 18, 1778," *P. C. C. Miscellany Folder 104,* No. 2827, Manuscript Division, Library of Congress.

10. *Journals of Congress,* 12:941; Deane to president of Congress, Sept. 22, 1778, Wharton, *Diplomatic Correspondence,* 2:737.

11. Examination of Carmichael concerning Silas Deane, Sept. 28, 1778, Ingraham, *The Case of Silas Deane,* Appendix X, p. 141.

12. Deane to president of Congress, Oct. 7, 1778, Wharton, *Diplomatic Correspondence,* 2:758.

13. Deane to president of Congress, Oct. 12, 1778, ibid., 2:768–68.

14. Ibid., 2:769.

15. Deane to president of Congress, Oct. 12; "Mr. Deane's Observations on Mr. Arthur Lee's Letter of June 1, 1778," ibid., 2:768–73, 773–77; Arthur Lee, *Observations on Certain Commercial Transactions in France,* report submitted to Congress (Philadelphia, 1780) Rare Book Collection, Library of Congress.

16. Deane to president of Congress, Nov. 19, 1778, Ingraham, *The Case of Silas Deane,* p. 128.

17. Deane to Barnabas Deane, Nov. 23, 1778, *Deane Papers,* 3:59–61.

18. *Journals of Congress,* 12:1181.

19. Deane to president of Congress, Dec. 4, 1778, Ingraham, *The Case of Silas Deane,* p. 131.

20. "To the Free and Virtuous Citizens of America," an address by Silas Deane, *Pennsylvania Packet,* Dec. 5, 1778.

21. Deane to Barnabas Deane, Dec. 7, 1778, *Deane Papers,* 3:76.

22. Laurens to Rawlins Lowndes, president of South Carolina, Dec. 7, 1778, Burnett, *Letters of Congress,* 3:520–21; *Journals of Congress,* 12:1202–6.

23. Ibid., 12:1200–1; Gérard to Vergennes, Dec. 10, 1778, *Despatches and Instructions of Conrad Alexandre Gérard, 1778–1880,* No. 62 (Baltimore, 1939) (hereafter cited as Gérard, *Despatches*); John Ettwein (contributor), "The Resignation of Henry Laurens, President of Congress, 1778," *Pennsylvania Magazine of History,* 13:(1889) 232–36; David D. Wallace, *The Life of Henry Laurens* (New York, 1915).

24. Lovell to R. H. Lee, Dec. 10, 1778, R. H. Lee, *Memoir of the Life of Richard Henry Lee, and his Correspondence with the Most Distinguished Men in America and Europe Illustrative of Their Character and of the Events of the American Revolution,* 2 vols. (Philadelphia, 1825), 2:145.

25. Arthur Lee to Bland, Dec. 13, 1778, R. H. Lee, *Life of Arthur Lee,* 1:-161.

26. "Senex" is supposed to have been Robert Treat Paine, a former delegate to Congress from Massachusetts; Almons, *American Remembrancer,* 7:371; *Pennsylvania Packet,* Dec. 15, 1778.

27. *Pennsylvania Packet,* Dec. 15, 1778.

28. Ibid., Dec. 17, 1778.

29. Ibid., Dec. 21, 1778.

30. Ibid.

31. Ibid., Dec. 29, 1778.

32. Ibid., Dec. 31, 1778.

33. Ingraham, *The Case of Silas Deane,* p. 17; *Deane Papers,* 3:204.

34. Reprinted in the *Pennsylvania Packet,* Jan. 19, 1779.

35. Deane to president of Congress, Jan. 4, 1779, Wharton, *Diplomatic Correspondence,* 3:9–10.

36. *Pennsylvania Packet,* Jan. 9, 1779; "To the Public" (rough draft), Jan. 7,

1779, *Papers of Robert Morris; Correspondence, 1775–1785,* No. 2148, Manuscript Division, Library of Congress.

37. *Pennsylvania Packet,* Jan. 12, 1789.

38. Ibid., Jan. 14, 1789.

39. Ibid., Jan. 23, 1789.

40. Ibid., Jan. 26, 1779.

41. Deane to president of Congress, Mar. 29, 1779, Wharton, *Diplomatic Correspondence,* 3:105.

42. Deane to president of Congress, April 26, 27, 1779, ibid., 3:139, 144.

43. Deane to president of Congress, Apr. 2, 17, 27, 30, May 22, 1779, ibid., 3:109, 118, 144, 148, 178.

44. *Journal of Congress,* 14:711–14.

45. Ingraham, *The Case of Silas Deane,* p. 98.

46. *Journals of Congress,* 14:929–30, 997–98.

47. Ibid., 14:929; Gérard to Vergennes, Aug. 8, 1779, Gérard, *Despatches,* No. 150; see entry of Aug. 5; Nov. 29, 1779, John Fell, *Diary in the Continental Congress,* No. 1392, Manuscript Division, Library of Congress.

48. Laurens to R. H. Lee, Aug. 10, 1779, Burnett, *Letters of Congress,* 4:358.

Chapter 8

1. Ingraham, *The Case of Silas Deane,* p. 77.

2. *Journals of Congress,* 14:997–98.

3. Laurens to R. H. Lee, Aug. 31, 1779, R. H. Lee, *Life of Richard Henry Lee,* 2:234.

4. Deane to president of Congress, Nov. 23, 1779, Wharton, *Diplomatic Correspondence,* 3:411–12.

5. Simeon Deane moved to Williamsburg, Virginia, and opened a store. In Dec. 1777 Simeon and Silas Deane formed the Simeon Deane and Company. The firm was not successful, and Simeon suffered from ill health. He died June 23, 1787, deeply in debt; Deane to William Duer, June 4, Deane to Simeon Deane, Aug. 4, Deane to James Wilson, Aug. 8, 1780, Deane to John Jay, Apr. 8, 1781, *Deane Papers,* 4:169, 177, 183, 298; Deane to Robert Morris, Sept. 2, 1780, Henkel, *Secret Correspondence,* No. 142, p. 71.

6.   Deane to Barnabas Deane, Apr. 20, 1780, *Deane Papers,* 4:130.

7.   Deane to Joseph Webb, June 2, 1780, ibid., 4:162–65.

8.   Morris to Deane, Mar. 31, 1780, *Deane MSS., CHS.*

9.   Morris to Franklin, Aug. 4, 1780, *Deane Papers,* 4:120–21.

10. Deane to Robert Morris, Aug. 4, 1780, Henkel, *Secret Correspondence,* No. 142, p. 71.

11. Deane to Isaac Moses, April 20, 1780, *Deane Papers,* 4:132.

12. Deane to Isaac Moses, Feb. 23, 1781, ibid., 4:279.

13. Deane to William Duer, Sept. 28, 1780, Deane to Simeon Deane, Sept. 29, 1789, ibid., 4:234–35, 237.

14. Deane to Moses, Aug. 9, Sept. 28, 1780, ibid., 4:188, 235.

15. Jay to Deane, Mar. 28, 1781, ibid., 4:294.

16. Deane to Wilson, May 11, 1775, ibid., 4:316.

17. Deane to Patrick Henry, Jan. 2, 1775, *Miscellaneous Collection,* Clements Library, University of Michigan; Deane to Samuel H. Parsons, Apr. 13, 1774, Deane, *Correspondence,* 2:129.

18. Deane to Thomas Adams, June 25, 1779, *Virginia Historical Magazine* 6 (1898):32.

19. Morris to Deane, Mar. 31, 1780, *Deane MSS., CHS.*

20. Deane to Wharton, May 10, 1780, *Deane Papers,* 4:146.

21. Deane to Wilson, Aug. 8, 1780, *Wilson MSS.,* Pennsylvania Historical Society, Philadelphia.

22. Aug. 21, 1780, ibid.

23. Deane to Shee, Sept. 4, 1780, *Deane Papers,* 4:220.

24. Morris to Deane, June 7, 1781, *Deane MSS., CHS.*

25. Deane to Wilson, Sept. 19, 1781, *Wilson MSS.,* PHS; Charles P. Smith, *James Wilson: Founding Father, 1742–1798* (Institute of Early American History and Culture, 1956).

26. Deane to Barnabas Deane, Sept. 13, 1781, *Deane Papers,* 4:464–65.

27. Deane to Wilson, Sept. 19, 1781, *Wilson MSS.,* PHS.

28. Arthur Lee to Committee on Foreign Affairs, Nov. 30, 1779, Franklin to William Carmichael, Mar. 31, 1780, Wharton, *Diplomatic Correspondence,* 3:416, 585–86; see also Bigelow, Franklin, *Works,* 7:19.

29. Franklin to Lovell, Oct. 17, 1779, Wharton, *Diplomatic Correspondence,* 3:384.

30. Franklin to president of Congress, Mar. 4, 1780, ibid., 3:536.

31. Franklin to Johnson, June 22, 1780, ibid., 3:809.

32. Deane to Morris, Sept. 2, 1780, Henkel, *Secret Correspondence,* No. 143, p. 71.

33. Deane to Jay, Sept. 18, 1780, *Deane Papers,* 4:230.

34. Deane to Johnson, Nov. 19, 1780, ibid., 4:260.

35. Deane to John Paul Jones, Nov. 21, 1780, ibid., 4:261.

36. Deane to Gérard de Rayneval, Dec. 9, 1780, ibid., 4:269.

37. Deane to Jay, Feb. 23, 1781, ibid., 4:277–78.

38. Deane to Simeon Deane, Feb. 23, 1781, ibid., 4:282–83.

39. Deane to Wilson, May 11, 1781, ibid., 4:318.

40. Deane to president of Congress, Mar. 29, 1779, Wharton, *Diplomatic Correspondence,* 3:104–6; Deane to Robert Morris, Sept. 10, 1781, Henkel, *Secret Correspondence,* No. 144, p. 71; No. 6, Record Group 39, Records of the Bureau of Accounts (Treasury) Fiscal Section, National Archives.

41. Deane to president of Congress, May 15, 1781, Wharton, *Diplomatic Correspondence,* 4:415.

42. Deane to Robert Morris, Dec. 10, 1781, Henkel, *Secret Correspondence,* No. 144, p. 71.

43. *Journals of Congress,* 21:995.

44. Ibid.; Deane to Frederick Grand, Dec. 24, 1781, *Deane Papers,* 4:554.

45. Deane to William Temple Franklin, Dec. 24, 1781, ibid., 4:554.

46. Deane to Barnabas Deane, Jan. 31, 1782, ibid., 5:31.

47. Deane to Barclay, Feb. 18, 1782, ibid., 5:64.

48. Barclay to Deane, Feb. 26, 1782, ibid., 5:69; see also "Mr. Deane's account with Mr. Barclay's observations . . ." No. 7, Record Group 39, Records of the Bureau of Accounts (Treasury), Fiscal Section, National Archives.

Chapter 9

1. All but two of the thirteen intercepted letters were written May 10 and June 15, 1781. Originally they were published individually by the Tory printer, James Rivington, in the *Royal Gazette.* Two letters addressed to Thomas Mumford and Barnabas Deane, dated September 24 and September 26, 1781, were delivered to the president of Congress on January 17, 1782, with unbroken seals. Congress voted to open and read the letters, but no action was taken except that it was ordered that an attempt be made to determine the authenticity of the letters and that American officials abroad be warned of Deane's apparent defection; Silas Deane, *Paris Letters, or Mr. Silas Deane's Intercepted Letters,* James Rivington, printer (New York, 1782).

2. Deane to Philip Schuyler, June 2, 1780, *Deane Papers,* 4:160–61; Arthur Lee to Theodoric Bland, Dec. 13, 1778, R. H. Lee, *Life of Arthur Lee,* 1:161.

3. Deane to Duer, Aug. 23, 1780, *Deane Papers,* 4:191.

4. Deane to Mumford, Aug. 28, 1780; Deane to Titus Hosmer, Sept. 1, 1780, ibid., 4:202, 210.

5. Deane to Jay, Sept. 18, 1780, ibid., 4:228.

6. Ibid., 4:229.

7. Deane to Jay, Oct. 10, Nov. 16, 1780, ibid., 4:245.

8. Beaumarchais to Vergennes, Dec. 2, 1780, *Archives Ministere des Affaires Étrangeres,* Vol. 13, translation in *Deane Papers,* 4:267.

9. William Lee to Arthur Lee, Dec. 10, 1780, William Lee, *Letters,* 3:835.

10. Dana to John Adams, Jan. 1, 1781, Adams, *Works,* p. 350.

11. Jay to Deane, Mar. 28, 1781, John Jay, *Correspondence and Public Papers,* ed. Henry P. Johnson, 4 vols. (New York, 1890), 1:445.

12. Deane to Jay, Apr. 8, 1781, *Deane Papers,* 4:296–301.

13. Jay to Deane, June 16, 1781, *Deane Papers,* 4:438.

14. George III to Lord North, Mar. 3, 1781, *The Correspondence of King George III with Lord North from 1768 to 1783,* ed. W. Bodham Donne 2 vols. (London, 1867), 2 (no. 669):363.

15. Clinton to North, Aug. 3, 1781, *Clinton MSS.,* Clements Library, University of Michigan.

16. George III to Lord North, July 17, Aug. 7, 1781, Donne, *Correspondence of George III,* 2 (no. 686):380 (no. 688):381.

17. Deane to Barnabas Deane, Oct. 21, 1781, *Deane Papers,* 4:506.

18. Deane to Barnabas Deane, Jan. 31, 1782, ibid., 5:23–31.

19. *Ibid., 5:31–32.*

20. *Ibid. 5:34.*

21. Livingston to president of Congress, Jan. 18; Livingston to Connecticut Governor Trumbull, Jan. 22; Livingston to Jay, Feb. 2, 1782, Wharton, *Diplomatic Correspondence,* 5:117, 123, 146.

22. Paine to Morris, Nov. 26, 1781, "Letters of Robert Morris," *New York Historical Collections* (New York, 1878), p. 471.

23. Madison to Pendleton, Nov. 13, 1781, Burnett, *Letters of Congress,* 6:262.

24. Madison to Pendleton, Dec. 11, 1781, James Madison, *The Writings of James Madison,* ed. Callard Hunt, 9 vols. (New York, 1900), 1:166.

25. Pendleton to Madison, Dec. 3, 1781, "Unpublished Letters of Edmund Pendleton," Massachusetts Historical Society, *Proceedings,* 2nd series (Boston, 1905), 19:143.

26. Wolcott to Andrew Adams, Jan. 2, 1782, Burnett, *Letters of Congress,* 6:284; see also Wolcott to Mrs. Laura Wolcott, Nov. 19, 1781, *Wolcott Papers,* CHS.

27. Everleigh to John Mathews, Jan. 22, 1782, Burnett, *Letters of Congress,* 6:296.

28. Secretary of Congress to Superintendent of Finance (Robert Morris), June 4, 1782, ibid., 6:363; Governor Trumbull to Robert Livingston, May 23, 1782, Wharton, *Diplomatic Correspondence,* 5:437.

29. Lee to James Warren, Apr. 8, 1782, "Warren-Adams Letters," *Massachusetts Historical Society Collections,* 2 vols. (Boston, 1917, 1925), 2:171.

30. Washington to Benjamin Tallmadge, May 15; Washington to Governor Trumbull, May 29, 1782, George Washington, *The Writings of George Washington from the Original Manuscript Sources, 1745–1799,* ed. John Fitzpatrick, 30 vols. (Washington, 1931–44), 4:259, 300.

31. Reed to Greene, Nov. 1, 1781, William B. Reed, *Life and Correspondence of Joseph Reed,* 2 vols. (Philadelphia, 1847), 2:373.

32. Tallmadge to Deane, Dec. 27, 1781, *Deane Papers,* 4:558.

33. Watson, *Men and Times of the Revolution: or, Memoirs of Elkanah Watson, Including His Journal of Travel in Europe and America, from the Year 1777 to 1842,* ed. Winslow C. Watson (New York, 1861), p. 151.

34. Livingston to Jay, Feb. 2, 1782, Wharton, *Diplomatic Correspondence,* 5:146.

35. Franklin to Livingston, Mar. 4, 1782, ibid., 5:216.

36. Barnabas Deane to Jacob Sebor, Nov. 11, 1781, *Deane Papers,* 4:531.

37. Simeon Deane to Deane, Nov. 14, 1781, ibid., 4:535; Burton J. Hendrick, "Worse Than Arnold," *The Atlantic Monthly* 156 (Sept. 1935):385–95.

Chapter 10

1. Deane to Jay, Feb. 28, 1783, *Deane Papers,* 5:137.

2. Beaumarchais to Vergennes, Dec. 2, 1780, *Archives Ministere des Affaires,* translation in *Deane Papers,* 4:267.

3. Franklin to Livingston, Mar. 4, 1782; Franklin to Morris, Mar. 30, 1782, Wharton, *Diplomatic Correspondence,* 5:216, 279.

4. Deane to Trumbull, Nov. 1, 1782, *Deane MSS.,* CHS.

5. Deane to Chaumont, Feb. 28, 1783, *Deane Papers,* 5:134.

6. Deane to Jay, Feb. 10, 1783, No. 17, Record Group 39, Records of the Bureau of Accounts (Treasury), Fiscal Section, National Archives.

7. Jay to Deane, Feb. 22, 1783, *Deane Papers,* 5:131.

8. Deane to James Wilson, Apr. 1, 1783, ibid., 5:148–52.

9. Deane to Barclay, Apr. 7, 1783, ibid., 5:154.

10. Deane to Barclay, Nov. 7, 1783, ibid., 5:228.

11. Deane to Beaumarchais, Apr. 2, 1784, ibid., 5:284–89.

12. Barclay to Morris, June 8, 1784, *P. C. C.,* pp. 54–49; Silas Deane, *An Address to the United States of North America,* (London, 1784); in 1784 Deane appealed to the American people in a pamphlet which with minor modification was a repeat of his 1778 "Address."

13. Morris to president of Congress, Sept. 30, 1784, *Deane Papers,* 5:323.

14. Deane to Washington, June 25, Deane to Jay, June 25, 1789, *Deane MSS.,* CHS.

15. Deane to Franklin, Oct. 19, 1783, *Deane Papers,* 5:212.

16. Deane to Morris, Oct. 10, 1783, ibid., 5:205.

17. Deane to Franklin, May 13, 1782, ibid., 5:90.

18. Deane to Franklin, Oct. 19, 1783, ibid., 5:213.

19. Deane to Jay, Jan. 21, Jay to Deane, Feb. 23, 1784, ibid., 5:279, 280; Jay, *Correspondence*, 3:114.

20. Allen to Shelburne, Jan. 10, 1783; Deane to Allen, Dec. 25, 1782, *Shelburne Papers*, 87:247, 249, Clements Library, University of Michigan.

21. Allen to Shelburne, Jan. 10, 1783, ibid., 87:247.

22. Deane to Franklin, Nov. 19, 1783, *Deane Papers*, 5:214–15; Sheffield, *Observations on the Commerce of the States* (London, 1782), Rare Book Division of the Library of Congress.

23. Deane to Simeon Deane, Apr. 3, 1784, Deane, *Correspondence*, 23:195.

24. Deane to Jay, May 3, 1784, *Deane Papers*, 5:299.

25. Sheffield to Deane, May 1, May 29, Sept. 22, 1783, Apr. 26, 1785, June 30, Sept. 26, Nov. 25, Dec. 26, 1788, Deane, *Correspondence*, 23:177, 179, 190, 209, 228, 232, 237; Sheffield to Edward Bancroft, Oct. 15, 1789, *Edith Bancroft Ashmore Collections*, Pennsylvania Historical Society, Philadelphia (hereafter cited as *Bancroft Collection*).

26. "Observations Respecting a Navigable Canal from Lake Champlain to the St. Lawrence," Deane to Dorchester, Oct. 25, 1785, *Canadian Archives*, ed. Douglas Brymner (Ottawa, 1889), series Q, 42:683; see also "Additional Observation Respecting a Navigable Canal from Lake Champlain to the St. Lawrence," Mar. 26, 1787, ibid., 22:693–706; see also Deane to John Foster, Oct. 28, 1783, Sheffield to Deane, Sept. 26, Deane to Sheffield, Nov. 25, 1788, Deane, *Correspondence*, 23:231, 228, 232.

27. Dorchester to Sydney, Oct. 24, 1787, *Canadian Archives*, 42:707.

28. Deane to Robert Morris, Oct. 10, 1783, No. 13, Record Group 39, Records of the Bureau of Accounts (Treasury), Fiscal Section, National Archives.

29. Deane to Sheffield, June 30, 1788, *Deane Papers*, 5:482–84.

30. Ibid.; Julian P. Boyd, "Silas Deane: Death by a Kindly Teacher of Treason?" *The William and Mary Quarterly 16 (1959), no. 2, 3rd series: 165–87; no. 3: 319–42; no. 4: 514–60.*

31. Deane to Barnabas Deane, Aug. 10, 1788, *Deane Papers*, 5:489; Deane to Bancroft, Saturday evening, 1788, *Bancroft Collection*, PHS.

32. Jefferson to Jay, Aug. 3, 1788, *The Papers of Thomas Jefferson*, ed. Julian Boyd, 15 vols. (Princeton, 1950), 13:463–68.

33. Jay to Jefferson, Nov. 25, 1778, ibid., 14:287–88.

34. Jefferson to Bancroft, Mar. 2, 1789, ibid., 14:605–6.

35. Jefferson to Jay, Mar. 15, 1789, ibid., 14:658–59.

36. Deane to Simeon Deane, July 25, 1783, *Deane Papers,* 5:183.

37. Langworthy to Deane, June 14, 1783, Deane, *Correspondence,* 23:181.

38. Morris to Deane, Dec. 5, 1785, *Deane Papers,* 5:471–72.

39. Sebor to Deane, July 1, 1785, Deane, *Correspondence,* 23:213.

40. Barnabas Deane to Deane, Sept. 28, 1788, ibid., 23:235.

41. Saltonstall to Deane, Nov. 19, 1788, *Deane MSS.,* CHS; Saltonstall to Deane, May 14, 1789, Deane, *Correspondence,* 23:238.

42. Barnabas Deane to Deane, Dec. 6, 1788, ibid., 23:235.

43. Jefferson to Madison, Aug. 28, 1789, Jefferson, *Works,* 15:368.

44. Peters to Deane, Aug. 12, 1789, Deane, *Correspondence,* 23:245.

45. "Obituary," *Gentlemen's Magazine,* 59 (Sept. 1789) part 2:866.

46. *American Mercury,* Dec. 28, 1789.

47. Barnabas Deane to Theodore Hopkins, Feb. 25, 1790, *Deane Papers,* 5:533.

48. Robert Herries and Co. to Jesse Deane, Jan. 7, 1795, Deane, *Correspondence,* 23:247.

49. John Webb to S. B. Webb, Dec. 6, 1789, Webb, *Family Letters,* 3:145.

50. Bancroft to Joseph Priestly, May 8, 1790, *Bancroft Collection,* PHS.

51. *Deane Papers,* 1:13; G. L. Clark, *Silas Deane, A Connecticut Leader in the American Revolution* (New York, 1913). The settlement of the claims may be followed in detail in the *Samuel Burch Papers: Papers Relating to the Claim of Silas Deane and his Heirs, 1775–1842,* No. 9126, Manuscript Division, Library of Congress. "Revolutionary Debts," 15th Congress, 1st Session, 1823 House Document, Series 9, No. 111; 20th Congress, 1st Session, House Document.

INDEX

Adams, John: and Jesse Deane, 88; and Silas Deane, 63; and foreign assistance, 29, 30; and foreign treaties, 23, 54; and Arthur Lee, 31, 62, 63; and Paris Commission, 26, 62; and war supplies, 5

Adams, Samuel: and Congress, 69; on Silas Deane, 7; and foreign assistance, 30; and foreign trade, 29; and Lee family, 32, 46, 47, 64

"Address," Silas Deane's, 76, 77, 79, 80

Allen, Andrew, 113

American Mercury, 120

American Revolution. *See* Revolutionary War

Amphitrite, 20, 43

Army, colonial, 5, 101; and French officers, 24–26, 64–65; and professional soldiers, 24; and supplies from France, 13, 17, 18, 19, 20, 34, 44–45

Atkins, John, 26

Arnold, Benedict, 69, 101, 102, 104, 112–13

Austin, Jonathan Loring, 132 n

Baltimore Advertiser, 84

Bancroft, Dr. Edward, 12, 21, 22, 32, 45, 116, 117, 120

Barclay, Robert, 96, 97, 104, 110–11

Beaumarchais, Pierre Augustin Caron de: and aid to American colonies, 15, 17, 18, 19–20, 42–43, 59; and Congress, 42–43, 96–97; and Silas Deane, 13, 14, 19–20, 27, 34, 43, 44, 60, 90, 100, 109, 111, 115; on Deane's recall, 57, 58–59; and Arthur Lee, 15, 18–19, 31, 32, 43, 58, 60; and Paris Commission, 34; and professional soldiers, 24,

25; and settlement of Deane's accounts, 111

Berkenhout, Dr. Joseph, 76, 78–79

Bermuda, 55

Bland, Theodoric, 46, 78

Bonvouloir, Achard de, 9

Boston Tea Party, 4

British West Indies, 114

Buck, Josiah, 1

Bunker Hill, 8

Burgoyne, John, 20, 48, 49, 111, 133 n

Burke, Thomas, 85

Canadian canal, 115

Carlisle Commission, 58

Carmichael, William: and charges against Silas Deane, 64, 71, 72–73, 101; and Silas Deane, 21–22, 32, 44, 66; and Benjamin Franklin, 49; and Arthur Lee, 21, 45, 47; and Paris Commission, 21–22, 47, 50

Chaumont, Monsieur de, 27, 32, 37, 44, 74, 90, 91

Choiseul, Duc de, 14

Clarkson, Matthew, 80

Clinton, Sir Henry, 103

Colonies, American: and alliance with France, 23, 47, 48–49; and British restrictions on commerce, 3–4, 8; and commerce with Great Britain, 8, 113, 114; and foreign assistance, 8–9, 28–29; and foreign trade, 23, 29, 30; and peace treaty with Great Britain, 109; and privateering, 22, 35–38, 39–40, 74; and supplies from France, 13, 17, 18, 19, 20, 34, 44–45. *See also:* Army, Colonial; Revolution, American

Commerce, American: with France, 23, 33, 47, 48–49; with Great Britain,

diers in American army, 24–25; and relations with U.S., 99; and supplies to Colonies, 18, 19, 20, 42; and treaties with Colonies, 45, 47, 48–49, 53–56

Franklin, Benjamin, 123 n, 132–33 n; and American privateering, 38; antialliance sentiments of, 23, 58; and Dr. Bancroft, 21; and Beaumarchais, 43; and British, 27, 49, 51, 52, 53; and Committee of Correspondence, 8, 12; and Silas Deane, 90, 93, 105, 107, 109–10, 112, 115; and Deane's recall, 57, 59, 61; on foreign assistance, 28–29; and French-American alliance, 49, 53–56; and French army officers, 25–26; and Ralph Izard, 73; and Arthur Lee, 31, 32, 38, 46, 57–58, 60–62, 75; and William Lee, 41; and James Lovell, 64–65; and Paris Commission, 11, 30–31, 32, 35, 64–65; popularity of, in France, 56; and settlement of public accounts, 61, 62, 93–94; and war supplies, 5

Franklin, William Temple, 32
French Foreign Office, 14
French War Ministry, 24
French West Indies, 55

Galloway, 123 n
Garnier, M., 16
Gentleman's Magazine, 120
George III, 21, 52, 102–3
Gérard, Conrad Alexandre, 82; and Silas Deane, 13, 46, 75, 92; and Benjamin Franklin, 52; and French-American alliance, 53–56, 74; as French minister to U.S., 59, 60, 61, 69; and Paris Commission, 73
Germain, George, 49
Grand, Monsieur, 27, 71, 75, 91
Great Britain: and American commerce restrictions, 3–4; and American maritime policy, 36; and American privateering, 36; and Anglo-French relations, 13, 36; and balance of power,

24; and Silas Deane, 27, 102–3, 104, 113; and France, 13, 36; and professional soldiers in colonial army, 25; and peace treaty with colonies, 109; and reconciliation efforts, 8, 23, 48, 49–52

Greene, Nathanael, 25, 107

Hancock, John, 71
Harrington, Samuel, 85
Harrison, Benjamin, 8, 44
Harwick packet, 37, 72, 73
Hessian soldiers, 8
Hodge, William, 37, 38
Hopkinson, Francis, 62
Hosmer, Titus, 68–69

Independence, Resolution for, 8
Indian trade, supplies for, 10, 12
Izard, Ralph, 51, 55, 62, 63, 73, 74, 93, 94

Jay, John: and army supplies, 17; and William Carmichael, 22; and Committee of Correspondence, 8–9; and Silas Deane, 20, 90, 91, 94, 95, 99, 101–2, 105–6, 109, 110, 111–12, 113; elected President of Congress, 78; on Lee family, 31; on mission to Spain, 22, 90, 91; and stolen Deane letters, 116–17
Jefferson, Thomas, 30, 116–17, 119
Jeffries, Dr., 116
Johnson, Joshua, 93–94, 95–96
Johnson, Thomas, 8
Jones, John Paul, 94
Journals of Congress, 67

Knox, Henry, 25

Land speculations, American, 91–92
Langworthy, Edward, 118
Lauraguais, Count de, 60
Laurens, Henry, 65, 69, 70, 76, 77, 78, 85
Lee, Arthur: and John Adams, 31, 62,